first light
last light

Dedication

This book is dedicated with love to my late parents May and Dick Naylor; our children Vicki and Steven; our grandchildren Sam, Ben and Kate; and our families the Naylors, Looneys, McPhersons, Dingles, Wooffindins and their offspring.

Special and warm thanks to the team at York Street for their guidance and inspiration – and thanks to Harry for carrying the tripod!

first light

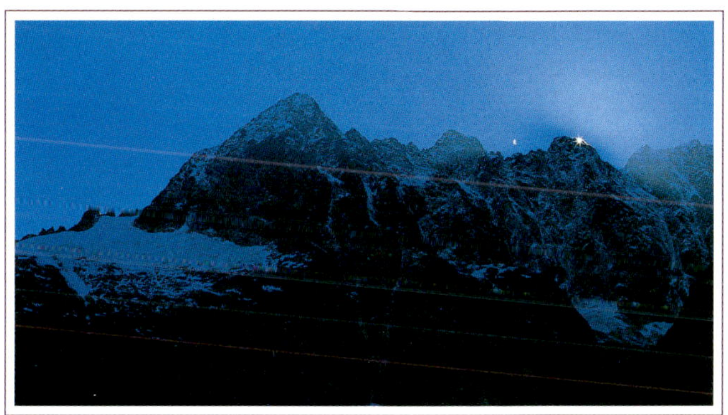

last light

photographs by fay looney

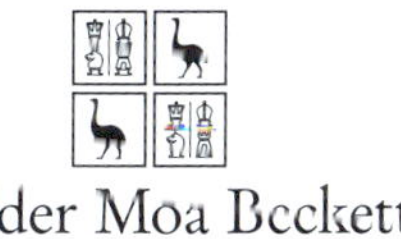

Hodder Moa Beckett

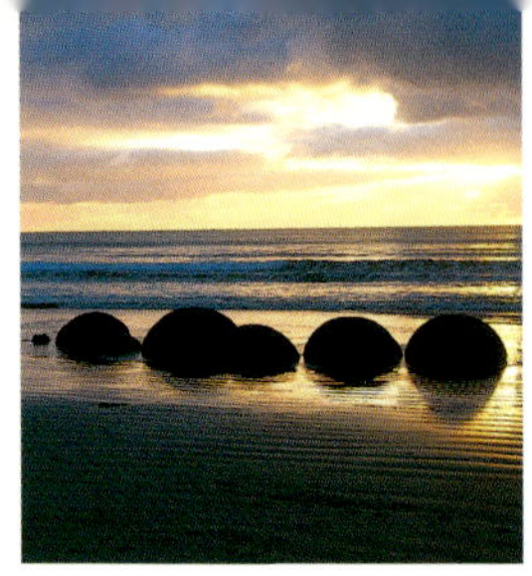

Contents

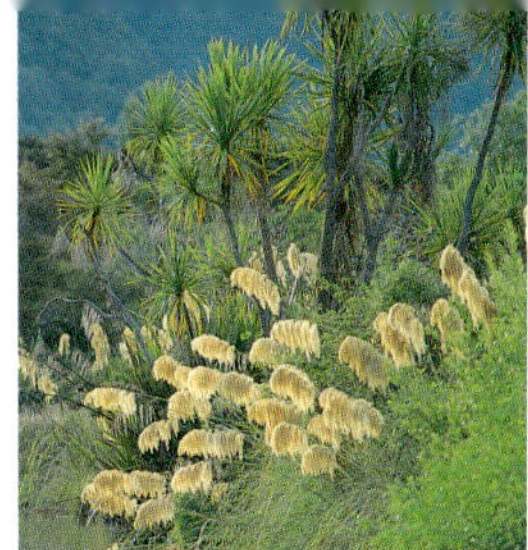

Introduction

To have a book published seems incredible to me. To make one about a place you grew up in and love to come home to is a joy. Photography is a bonus in my life thanks to my mother, May Naylor, who, 24 years ago, insisted I answer an advertisement for a school photography salesperson. And so it happened – I finished selling and started as a photographer. I learnt to see and capture the beautiful New Zealand light as I travelled the country.

At four in the morning in April 1987 I found myself standing on Westminster Bridge holding a film back for photographer and friend Nick Servian from Wellington. As the dawn arrived, Nick in his humorous way said, "Do you know the difference between a good shot and a bad shot?"

Yawning, I said, "Tell me."

"The time you get out of bed in the morning," he answered.

My landscapes improved from then on.

This book is about mornings and late evenings in different parts of New Zealand and the memories they evoke of my late parents who always encouraged their four daughters to enjoy and explore the space we lived in. Many of the photographs take me on a personal trip back to great family times spent fishing and camping in places our grandchildren now enjoy. Many are new discoveries about the way light colours and shapes the landscape.

I live under Mount Taranaki on the West Coast of the North Island and, along with the ocean, this is my favourite subject. I'm inspired by the sight of morning sunlight brushing the mountain with apricot hues and bringing the crater into sharp focus. I watch as the light deepens the blue of the Tasman Sea and accentuates the green dairy country. In the evening, the sun settles into the ocean outside my window and casts warm, red, pink and mauve tones on the water. It turns the winter snow shades of cerise.

First light has rewarded me with many breathtaking moments as I wait on a cliff top or a beach for it to shape the land. This collection of images is about some of these moments. Last light is when I shoot many of my portraits bathed in the "cape light", which is warm and flattering to skin tones, while showing the beauty of the landscape we live in.

Every shot appears as nature coloured it and, as my friend Anne says, "Nature never gets it wrong." I remember her comment often as I watch water turn gold and red.

First light drew me to the Chathams, a place I knew nothing about, which is now the focus of world attention as the new millennium approaches. The dawn light we enjoy on the mainland arrives 45 minutes earlier in the Chathams and brings with it dancing rainbows, clear beautiful days and starlit nights.

Autumn in Southland and Otago was perfect and my introduction to Macetown and Skippers was also a highlight. I marvelled at the energy and vision of the early settlers as we followed their trails into the goldfields. The fact that I timed my last trip to coincide with the opening of the oyster season at Bluff and the crayfish season in the Chathams was a mouthwatering fluke. If I could give you the taste of a Bluff oyster, a Chathams crayfish, West Coast whitebait and Waihaha fresh smoked fish – I would.

Because there is still so much of this land to explore, I carry my camera with me every day. I hope the photos in this book communicate my love of the New Zealand land and sea and, like the first light in them, brighten the new day.

Fay Looney

Fay Looney
August 1999

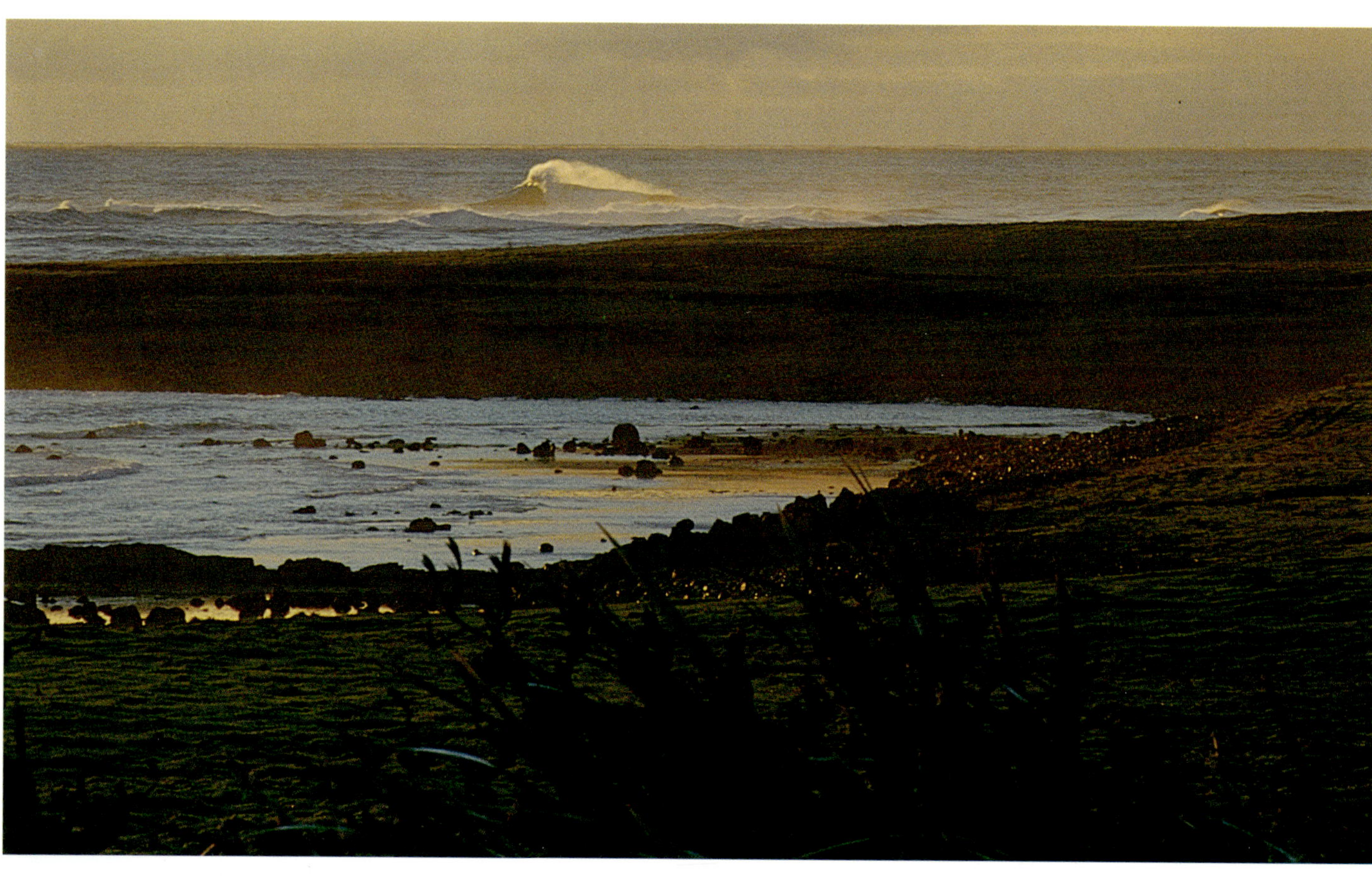

Pitt Strait,
Chatham Islands

Millennium mile. Pitt Island is where the sun will rise first on inhabited land in the year 2000. If they have to wait as long as I did to get a shot it could be a while before anyone gets to drink the champagne. The wait is made easy by watching the force of the opposing oceans meeting on the Owenga coast and the bird life on the beach below.

Waitangi, Chatham Islands

The Chatham Islands welcomed us with this ever-present rainbow. It danced its way ahead of us on the bus trip from the airport to Waitangi. The commentary, narrated by the driver's young son over the speaker system as we drove, was very entertaining. "That's Uncle Hori's place; there's the golf club, but sometimes they have parties there." I was delighted to meet the rainbow again the following morning, along with the young boy who always gave us a wave.

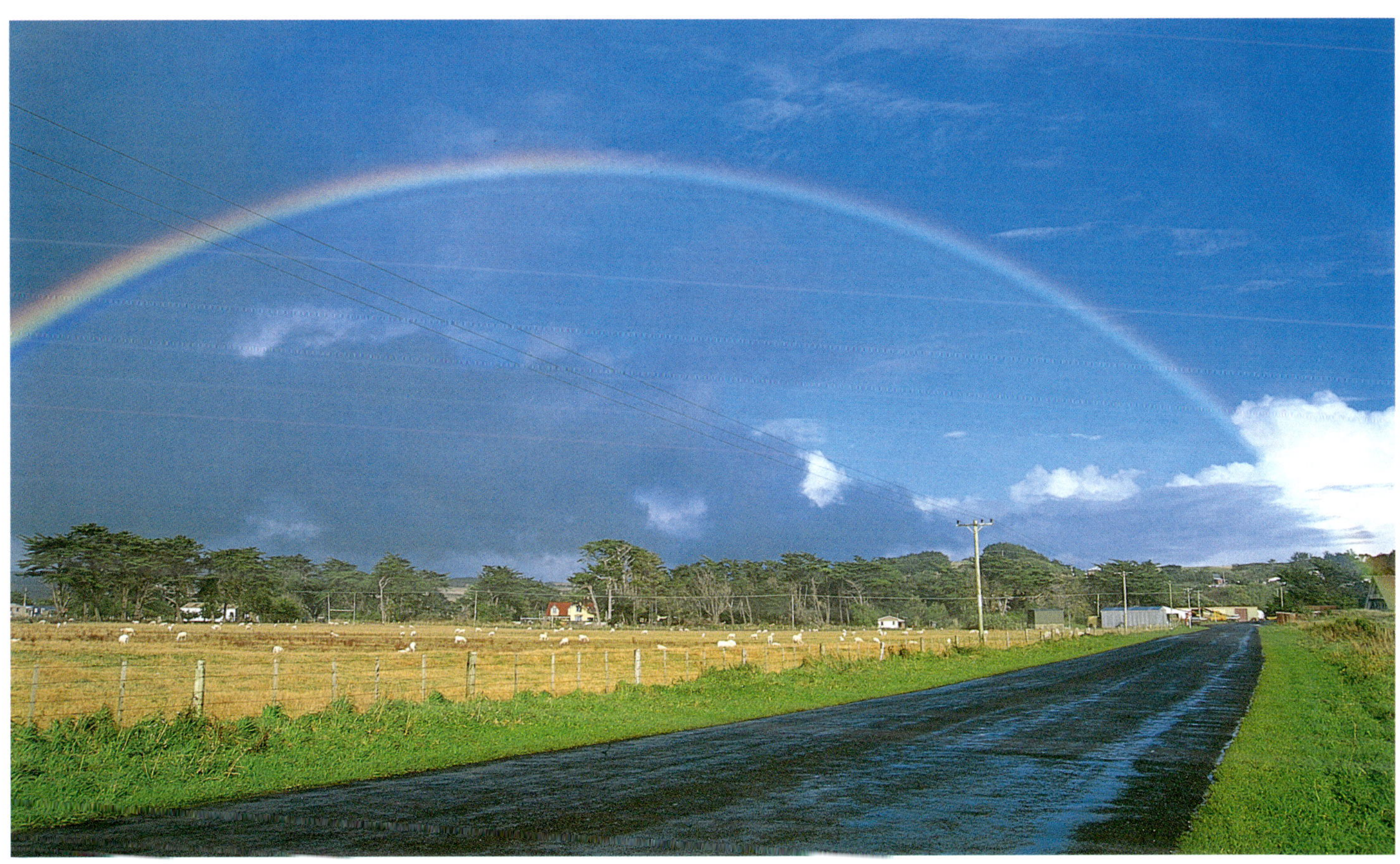

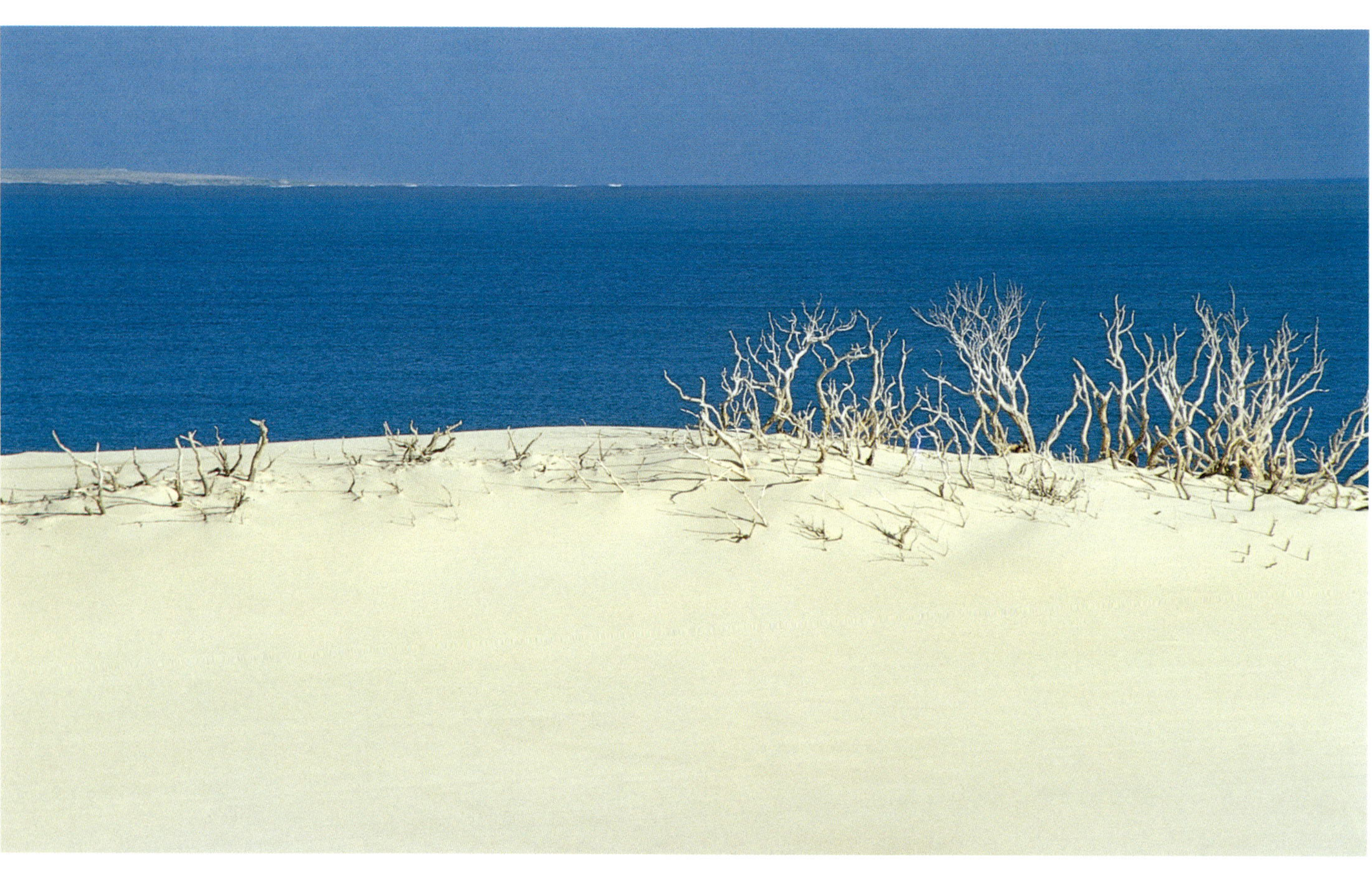

The Sand Blow, Chatham Islands

The exotic face of the Chathams is unexpected. We saw stretches of white, sandy beach sometimes mixed with black volcanic sand and watched as cattle fed on the kelp scattered at the high tide mark. I hope millennium fever doesn't change the island – there are some places on earth that should stay the same and this is one.

Land Apart They Call It

Raw and real Chatham Islands,
  unmuffled cars rattle you awake.
White ocean spray shreds the red cliffs of Waitangi Beach.
Showers coloured by rainbows seem within reach,
  nature-sculptured lagoons and peaks.
Distressed trees bleached by the salt bend in the dunes,
  cattle wander beaches sampling the kelp.
Shipwrecks there are many, long beyond help.
Black gold from the sea brings smiles to the faces
  with stories of deep and lonely places.
This place is special – it shows on the warm face of its people.
Folk attached to the land by choice,
  with children who wave to strangers like me.
The first light is coming and with it the fame.
Like a rainbow, may it touch and leave this land in peace again.

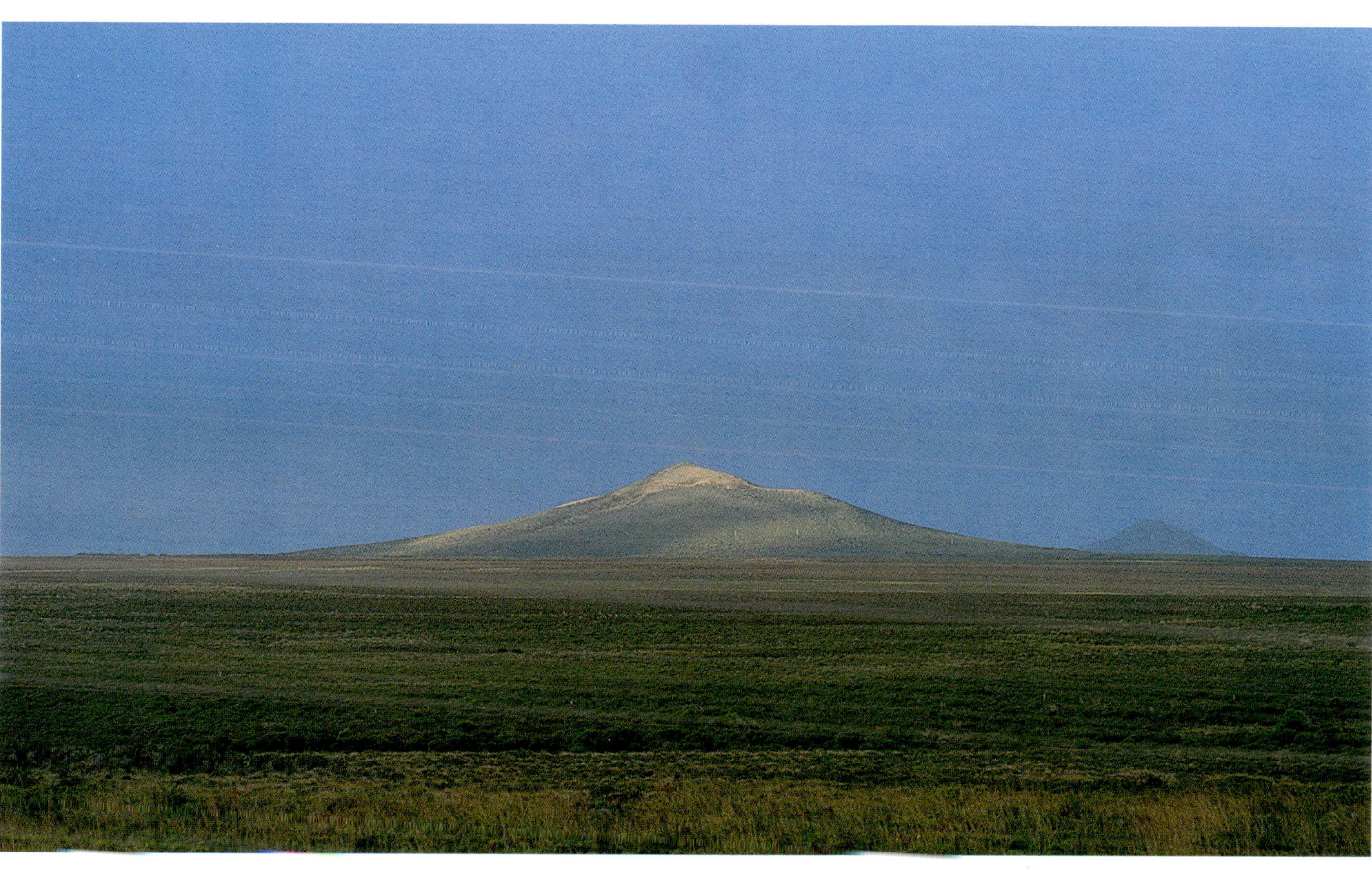

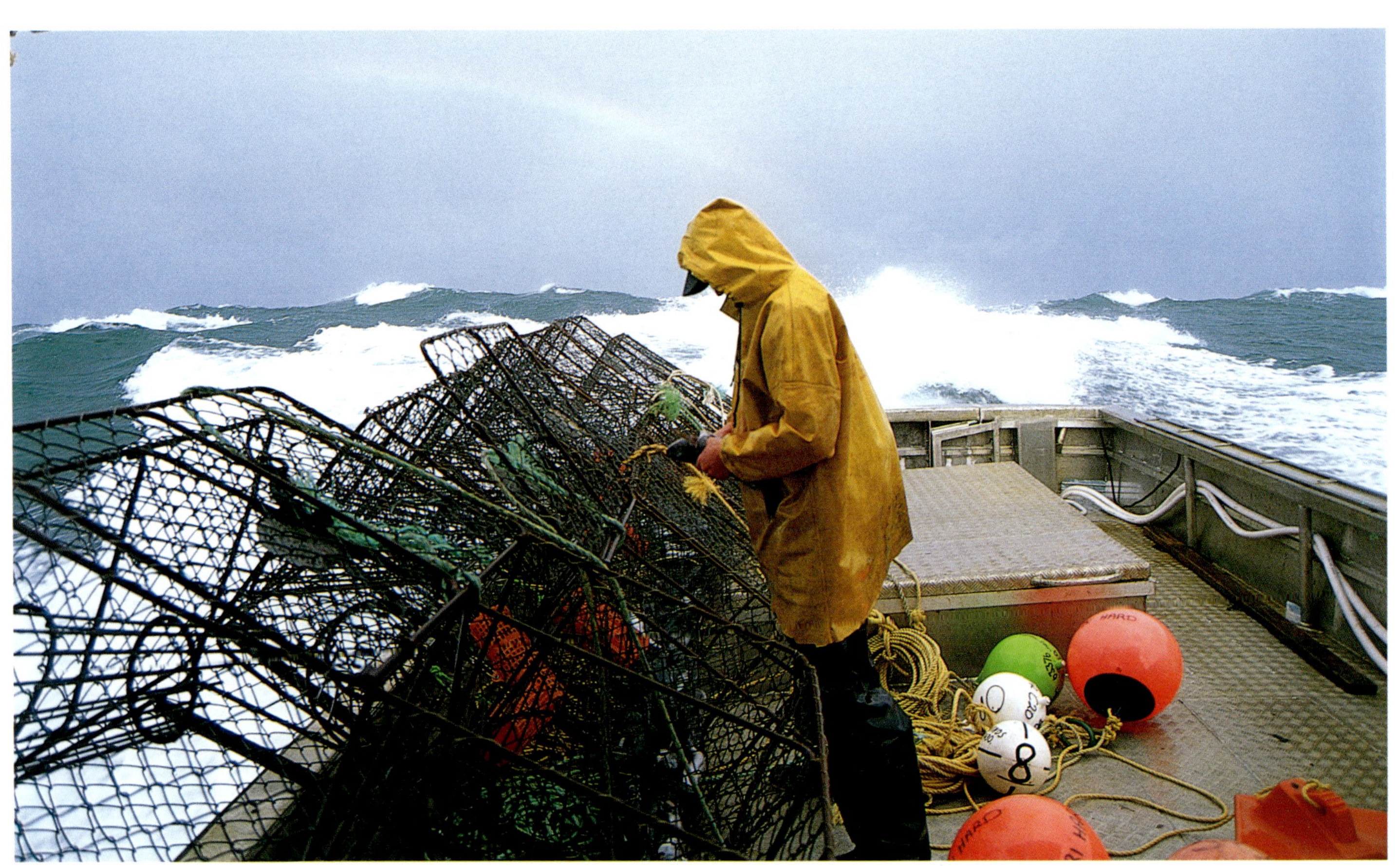
HARD

Port Hutt, Chatham Islands

A very painful shot. I broke my leg as we rode the surf to retrieve these cod pots and lay on my back in the bottom of the boat until it turned and ran with the sea. The young deckhand rode the boat easily as he emptied the pots and then returned them to the white-capped ocean. Clarkey, the unrepentant skipper, felt I should get a shot, so this is it.

Hokianga

Hokianga is a spiritual place of mist and water. High in the hills above Kohukohu, the morning after I was introduced to our new grandson Ben, I walked to a point where I could see across the hills and watched the clouds form and lift out of the deep canyons. It's always a surprise to me to capture cloud on film because it seems so elusive.

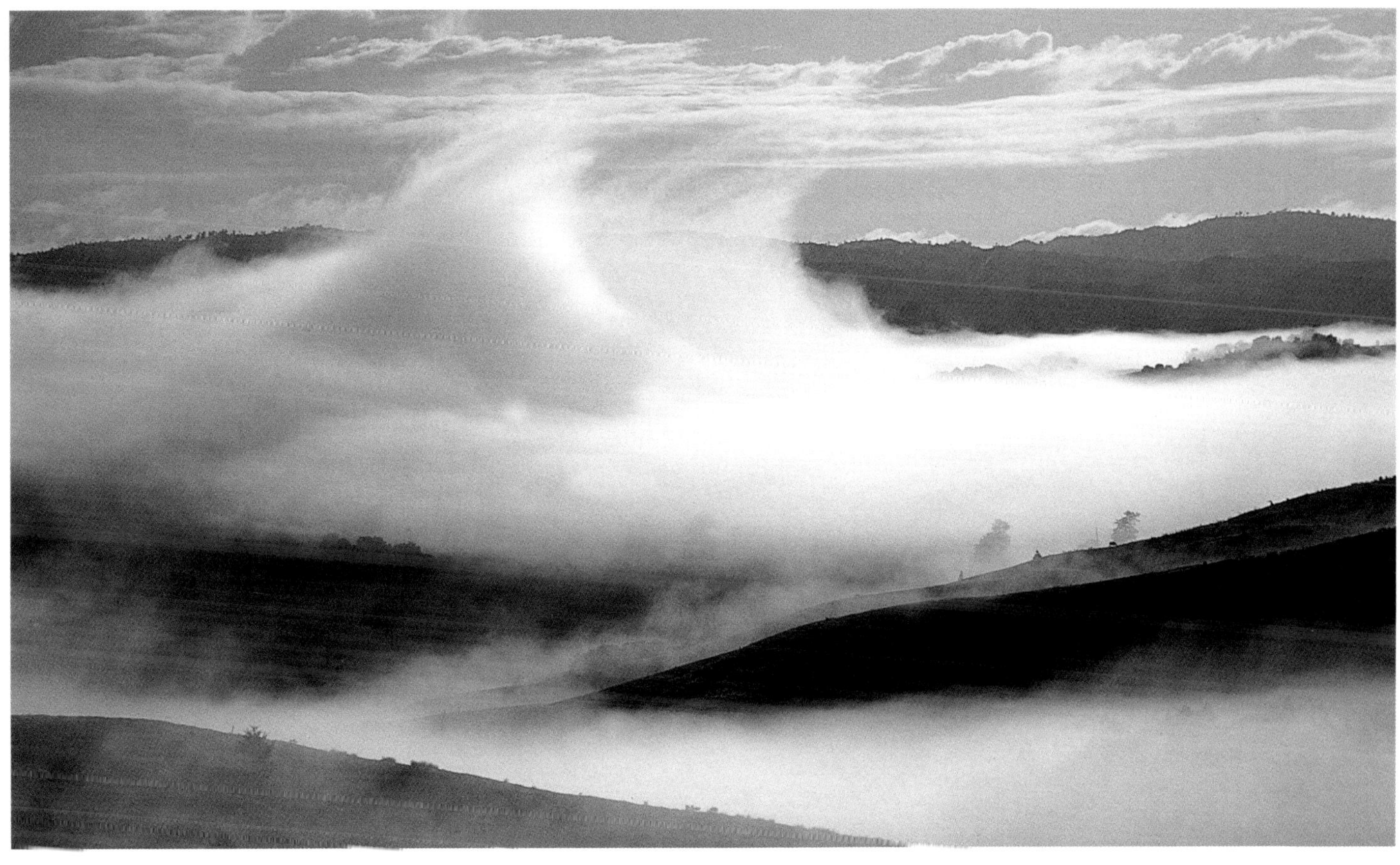

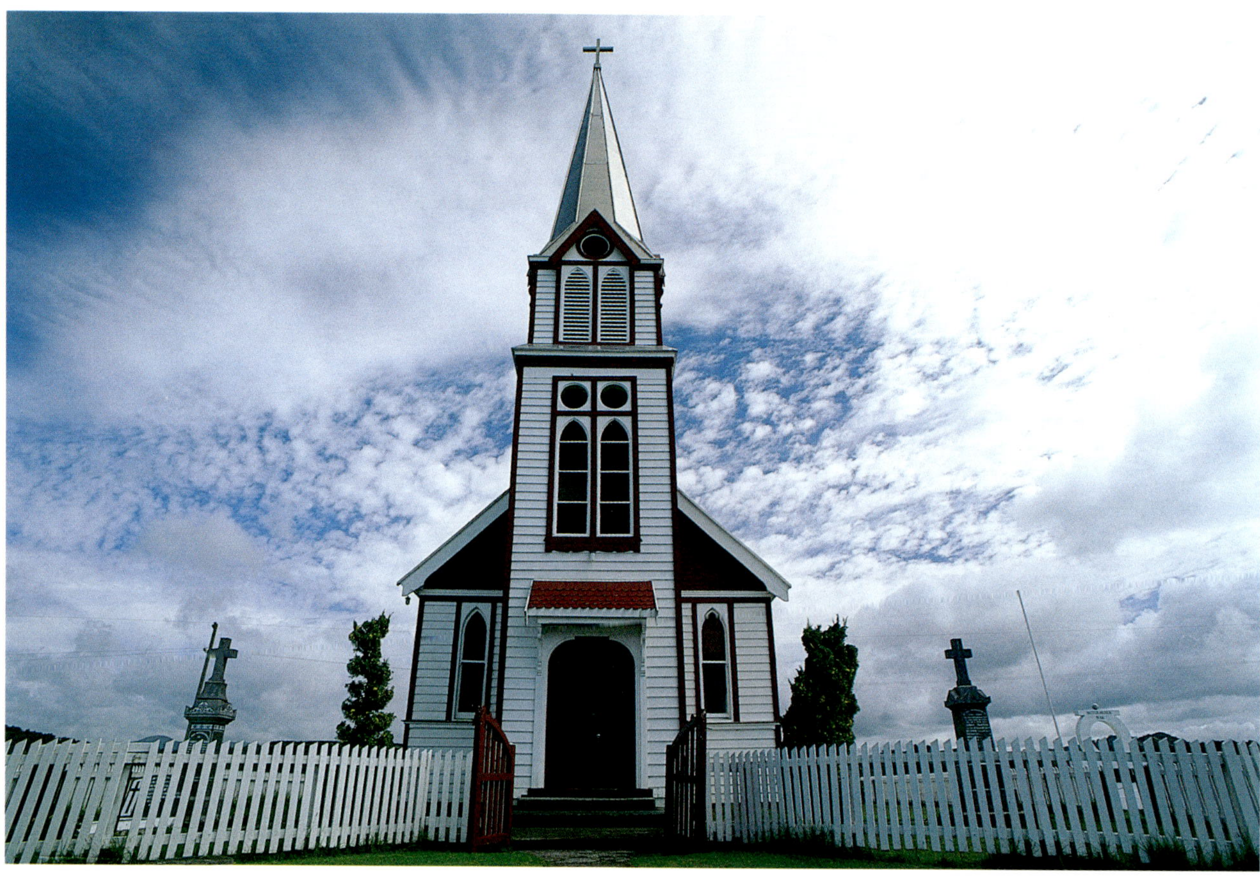

Motukaraka

Looking across from Rawene, as you wait for the car ferry, Motukaraka Church dominates the skyline. We farewelled a young friend in this beautiful church and felt humbled by the aroha (love) in this place of Kupe's return. I love the clouds that seem to have been speared by the steeple.

Waimamaku

After leaving the Waipoua Forest in the rain, we came across this perfect rainbow lifting the gloom of Northland floods and pouring rain in Waimamaku. Capturing it on film was the easy part but keeping the camera dry was difficult.

This shot is special and it's for Mum and Dad, who loved rainbows, and us.

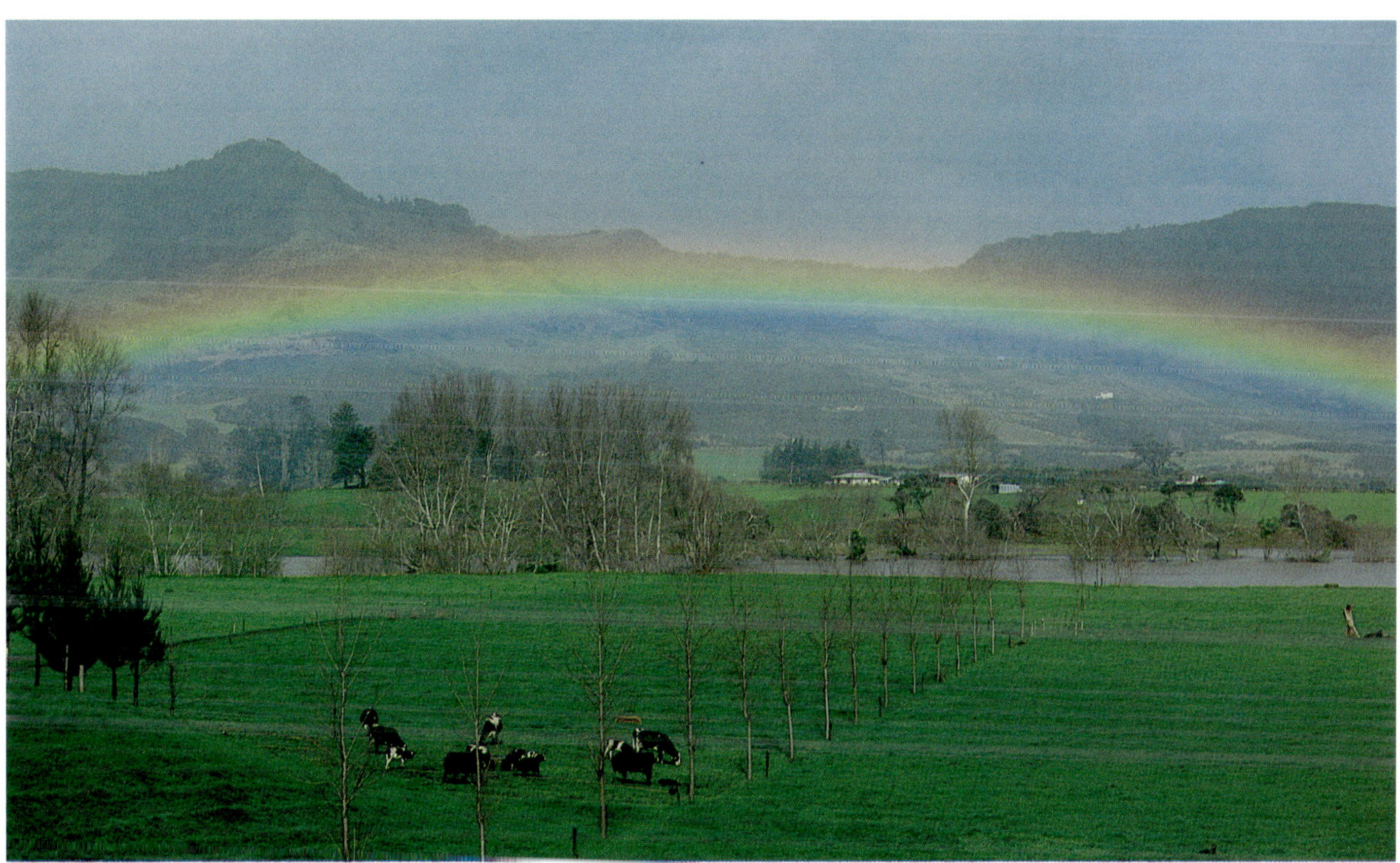

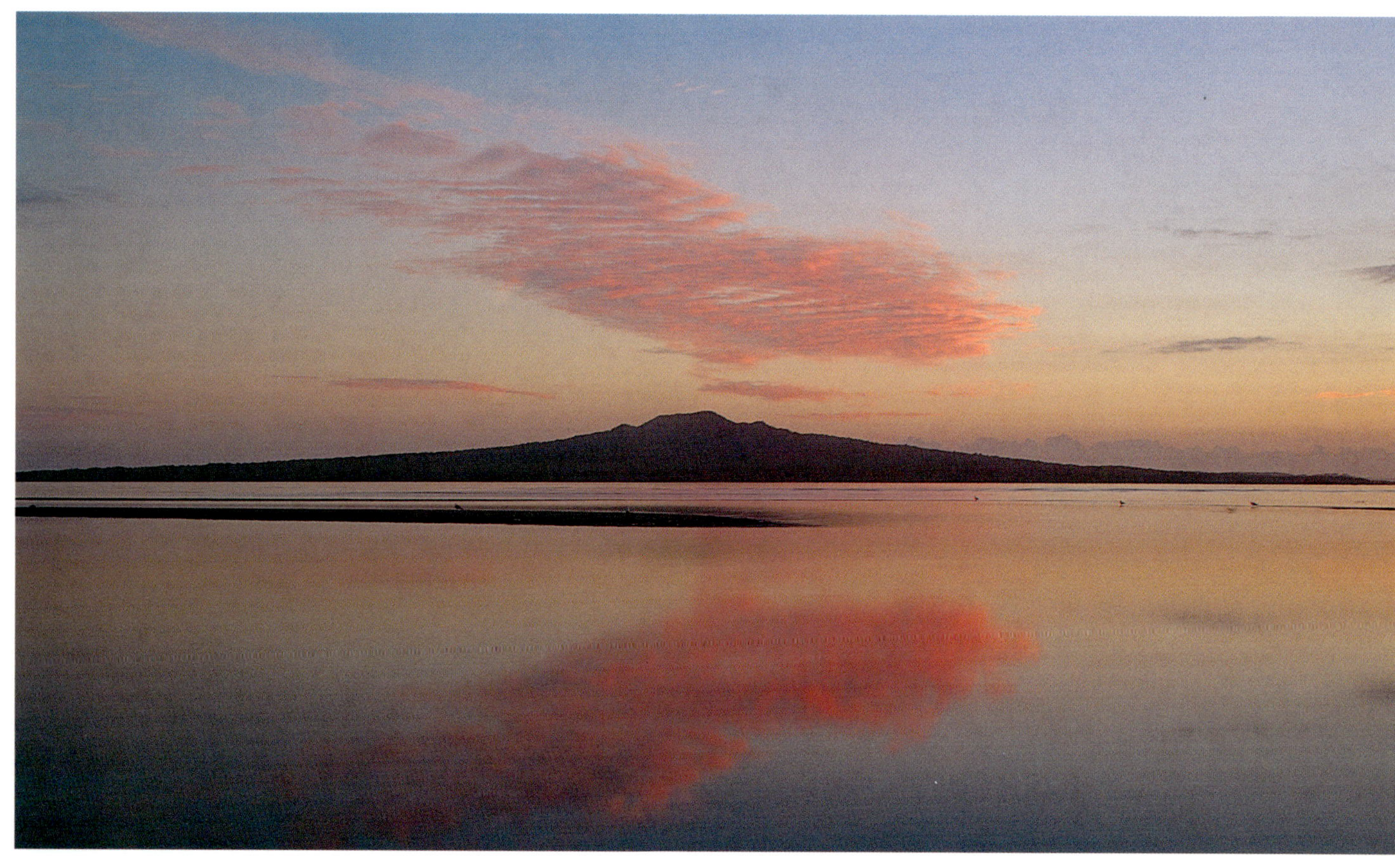

Rangitoto

A view of Rangitoto from Cheltenham Beach at daybreak. People jogged past me in the dark, surprised to see me standing in the water, but the dawn showed them that I really did have a reason for doing so. Someone was watching over me for this shot as I only had one chance at it before I moved on. I think it was my dad, who regaled me with many stories of his childhood and the wallabies that lived on Rangitoto Island.

Westhaven

Westhaven is such an interesting place in the early hours – busy with joggers and security people. Just for a few moments the craft seem to take a breath before the day starts and the lights turn off. The masts number in their thousands now and the big one in the middle reflects the rapid changes that have taken place.

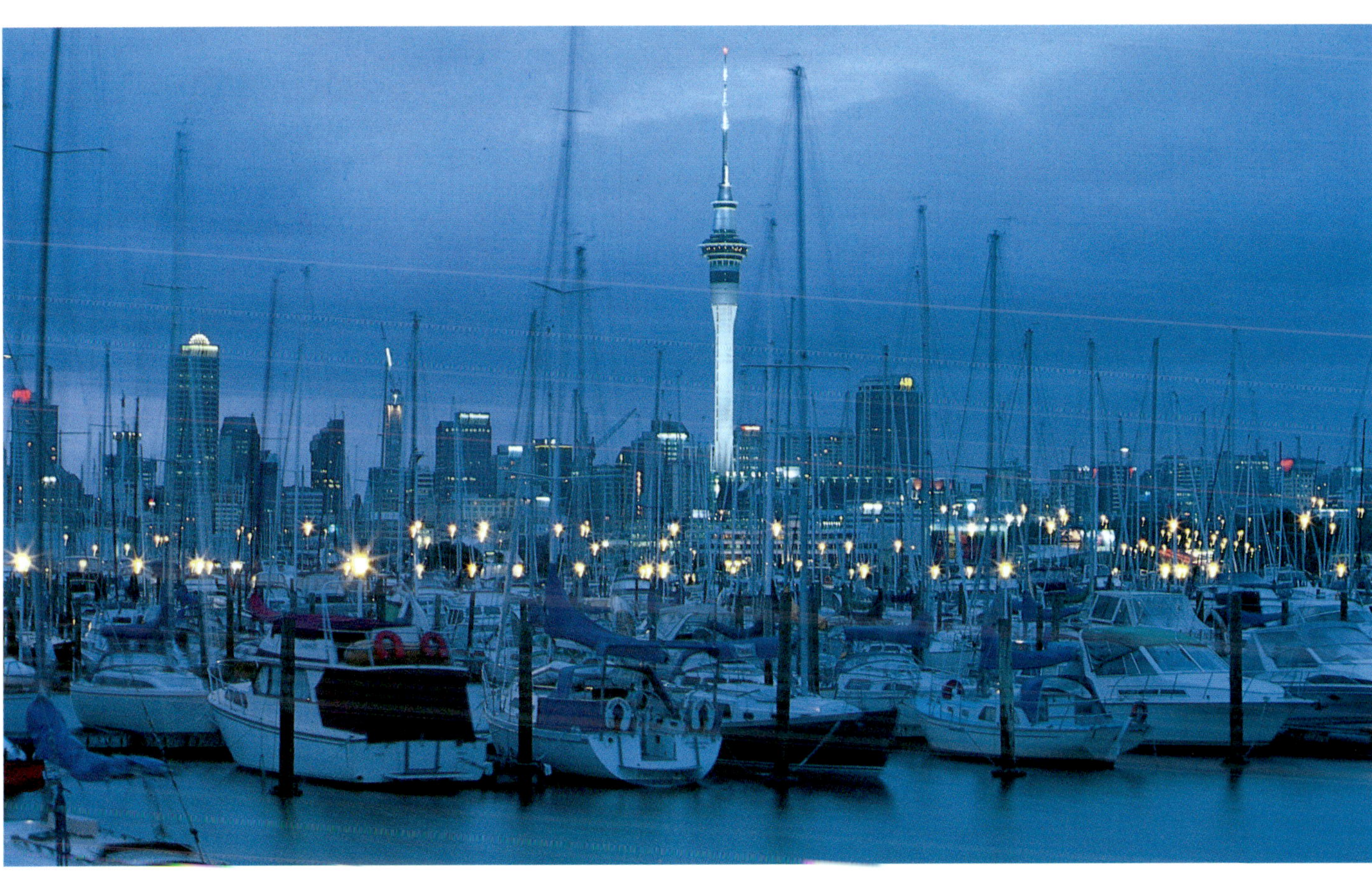

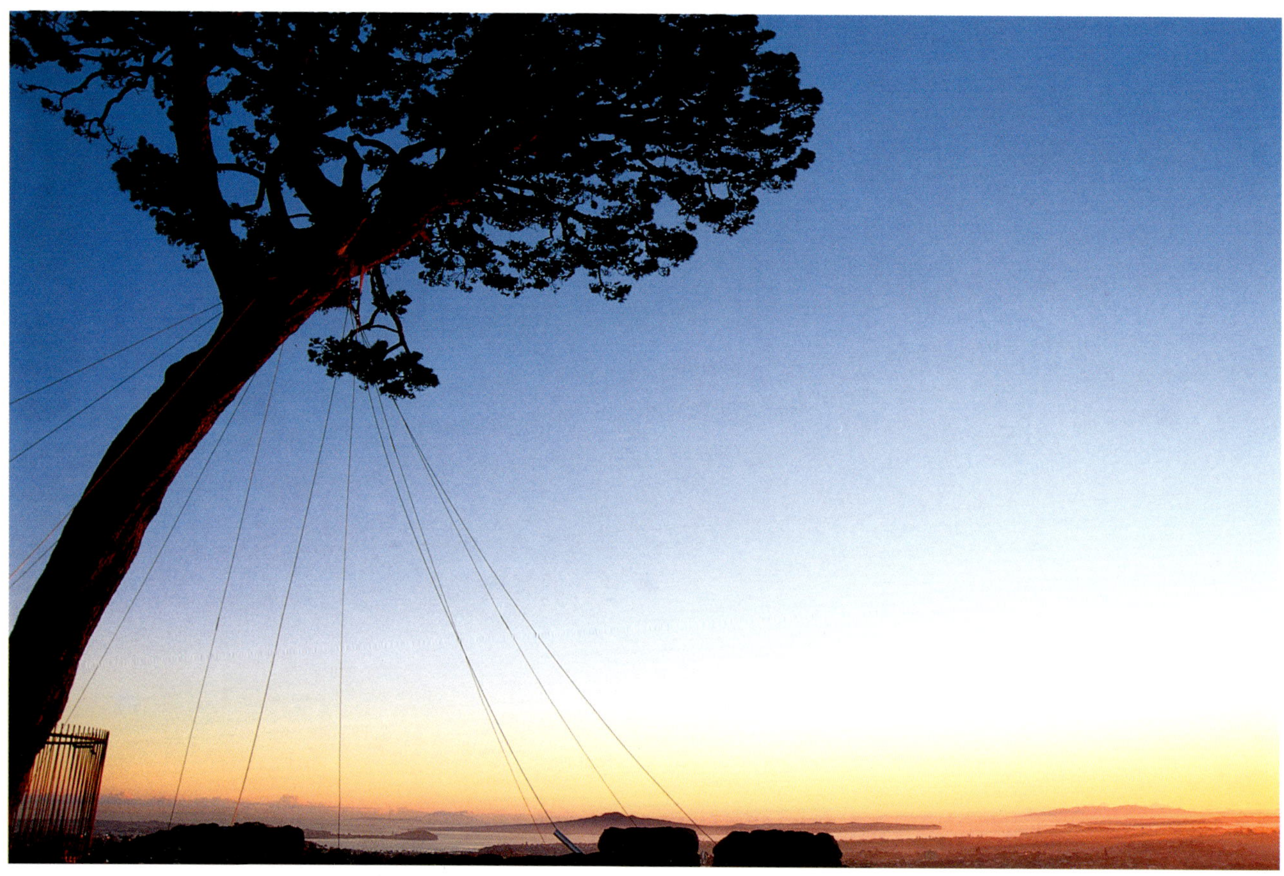

One Tree Hill

Early morning on the summit of One Tree Hill offers a peripheral view of Auckland city, and it's a great place to walk the dog, as many folk do. The wire cage and ropes supporting this lonely pine on Auckland's skyline, seem softened by dawn's early light. The hard steel softens into a spiderweb.

Lake Taupo

Harry fishing as dawn breaks over the Waihaha ripple. This is heaven on earth for those who enjoy fly fishing even half as much as my husband and most of my family. This well-known spot has even been fished by members of the Royal Family including Prince Charles and the Queen Mother. This is the best time to catch a rainbow trout – if he doesn't catch anything in the next few moments it's all over. We only need one fish for breakfast and if he catches more, the rest will be thrown back.

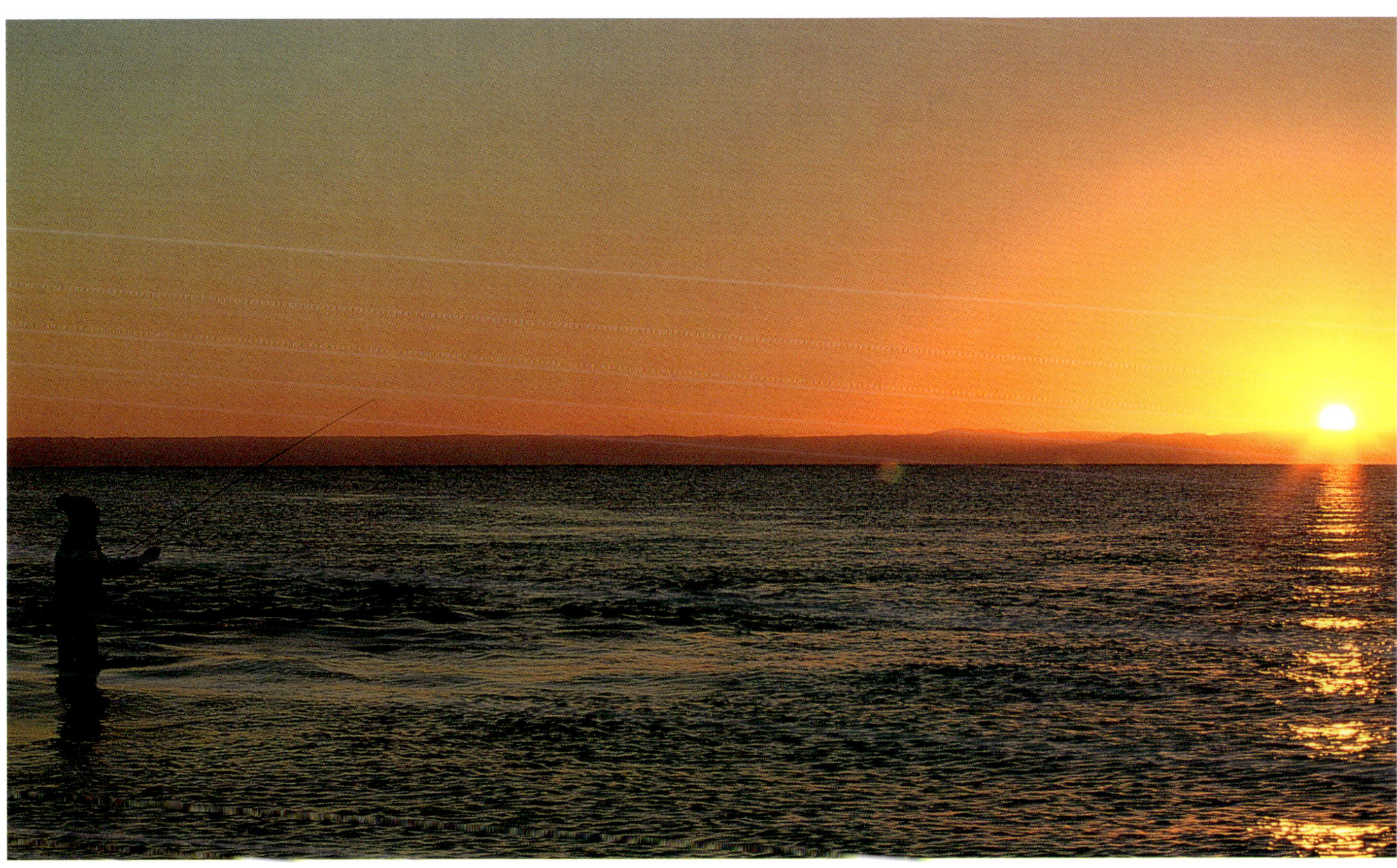

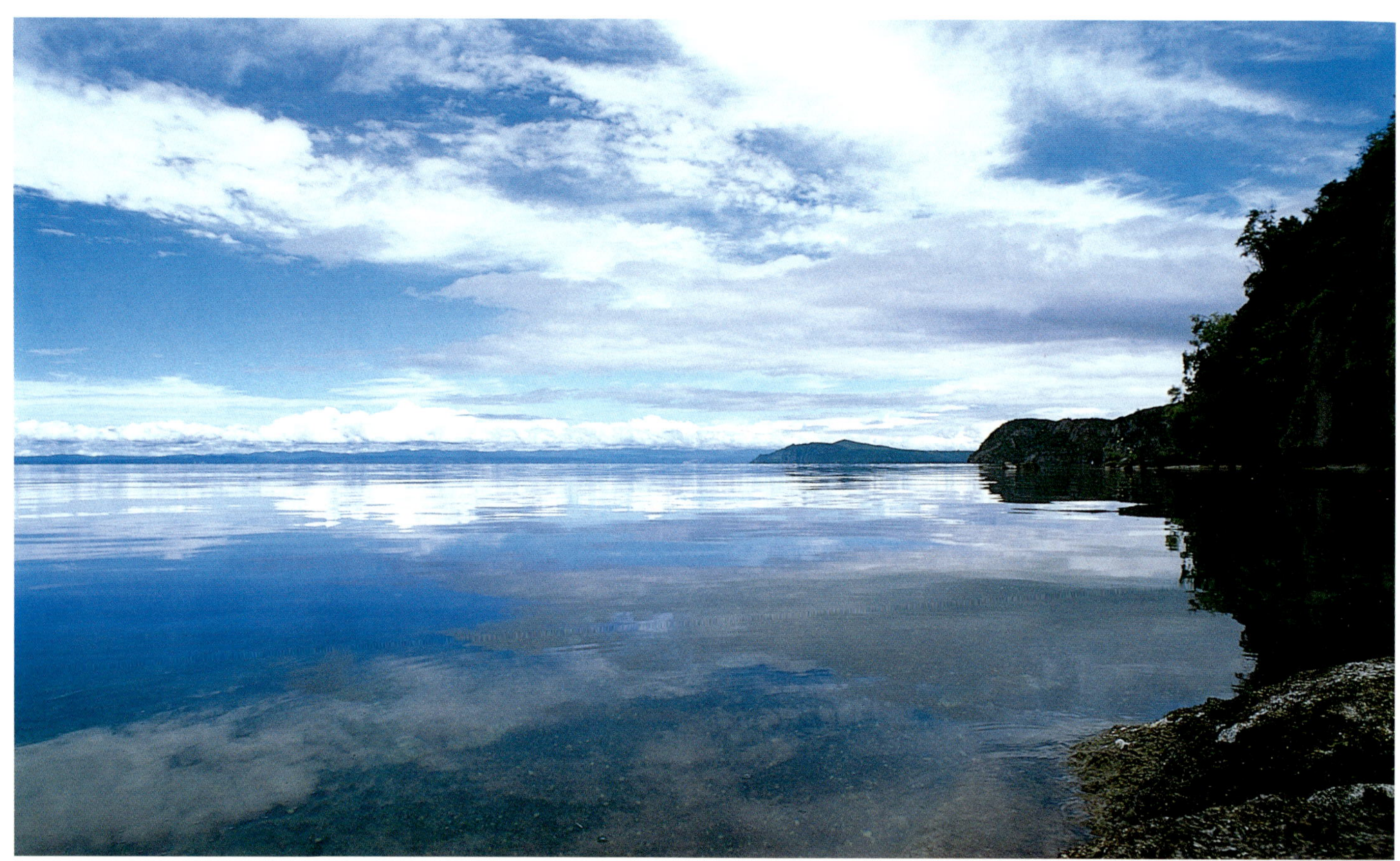

Kotutuku Bay, Lake Taupo

How many places on earth can you drink the water you swim in? One of them is Kotutuku Bay, Taupo, also affectionately known as Twin Bays to those of us who rush there early in the morning hoping to be there first so we can skinny dip before breakfast. The clouds skip by and reflect the peace we feel in this idyllic spot.

Waihaha River

I often see this view as I sit on our boat anchored on the spit at Waihaha in the Western Bays of Lake Taupo. I've watched many swans giving flying lessons to their young at first light on this patch of water. The toi toi offers shelter to many water birds and shadow for the brown trout that live here.

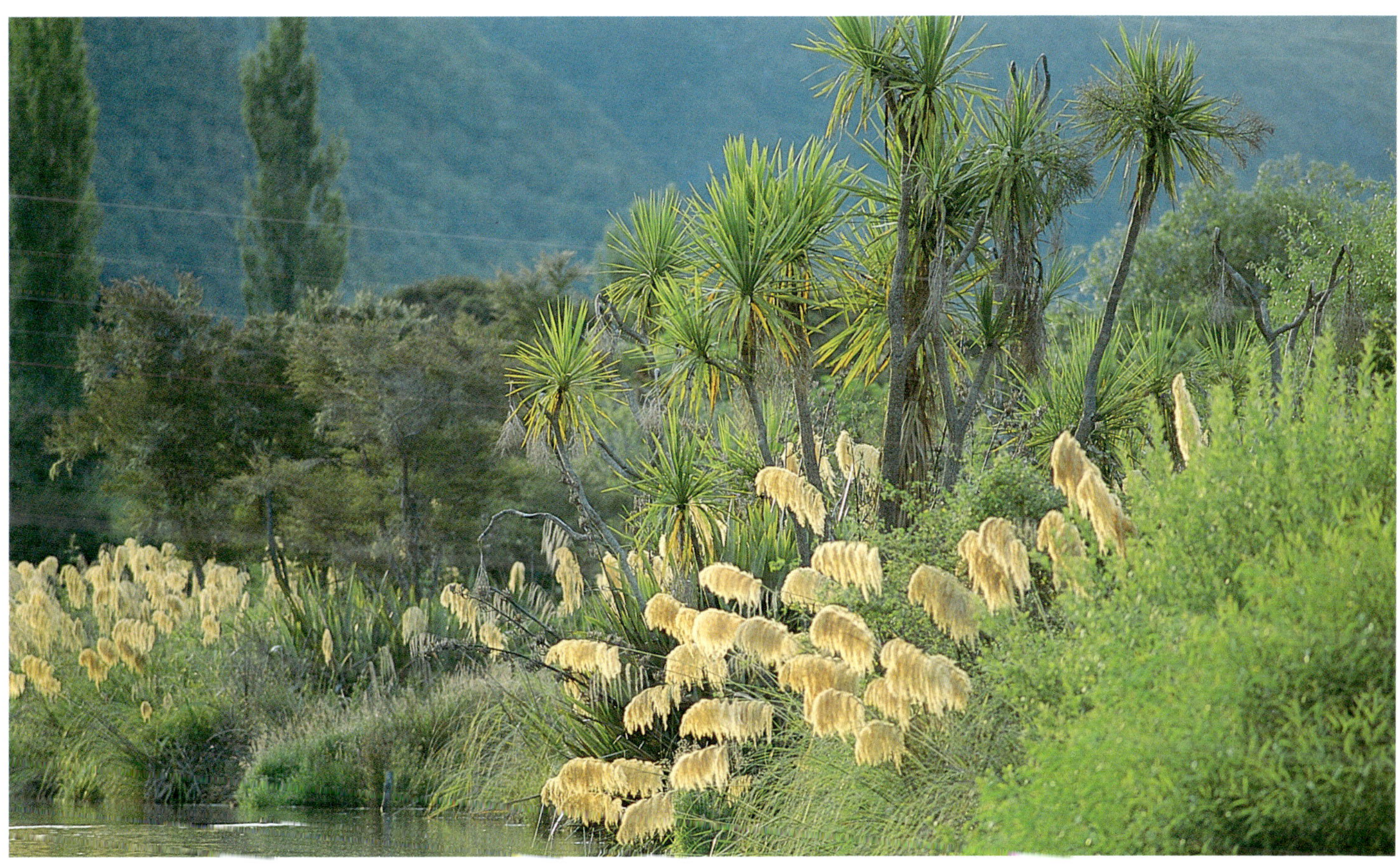

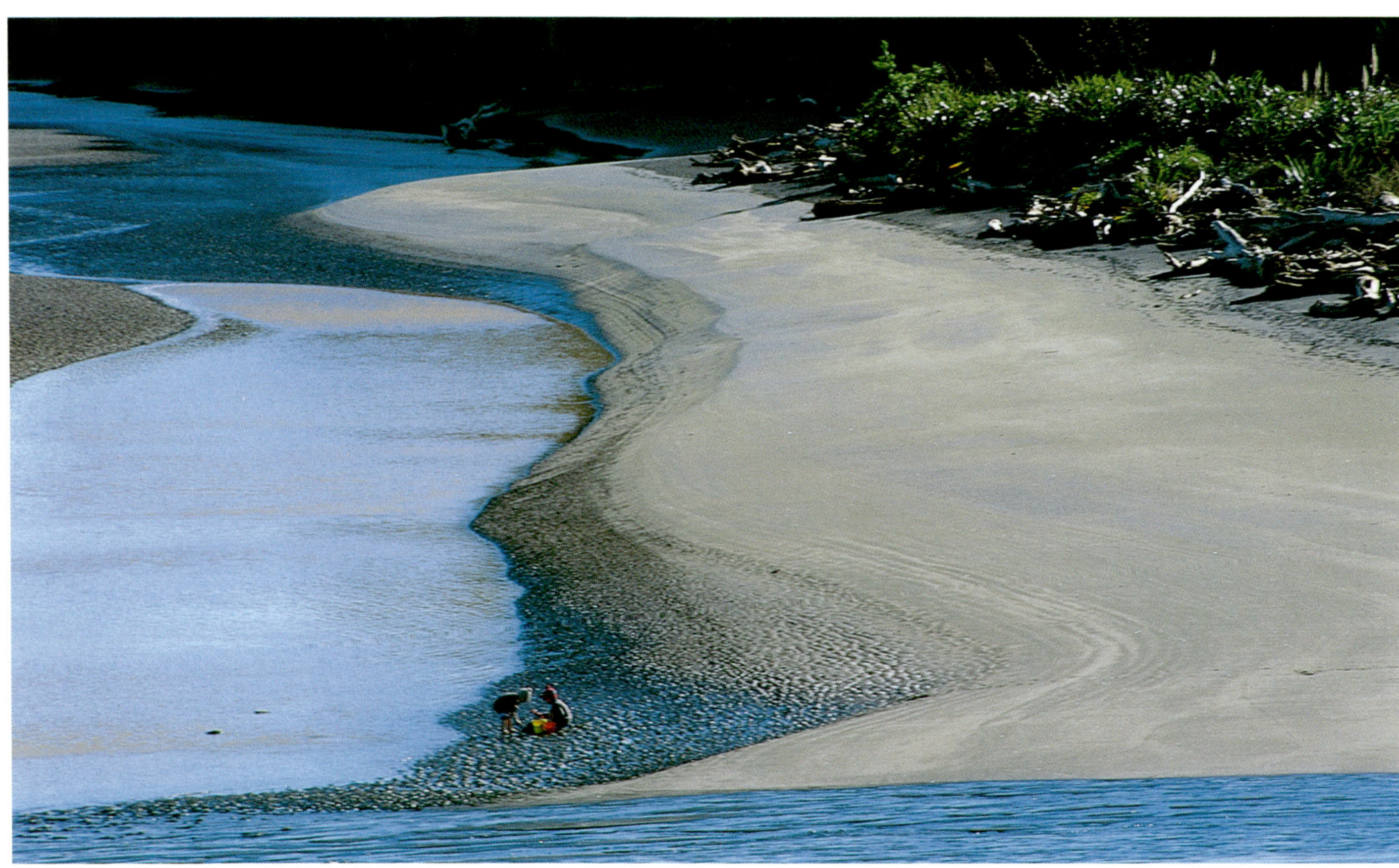

Awakino Heads

Two children play while their parents fish for whitebait nearby in this corner of the Awakino River mouth. The black sand rippled by the tide and the blue sky arc both caught by early light which gives the scene a graphic quality.

Tongaporutu

This image was taken on the cliff tops above Tongaporutu at the beginning of the Pukearuhe, Whitecliffs Walkway. The setting sun turned the sea gold for a split second and, fortunately, I was looking through the lens and able to grab the moment.

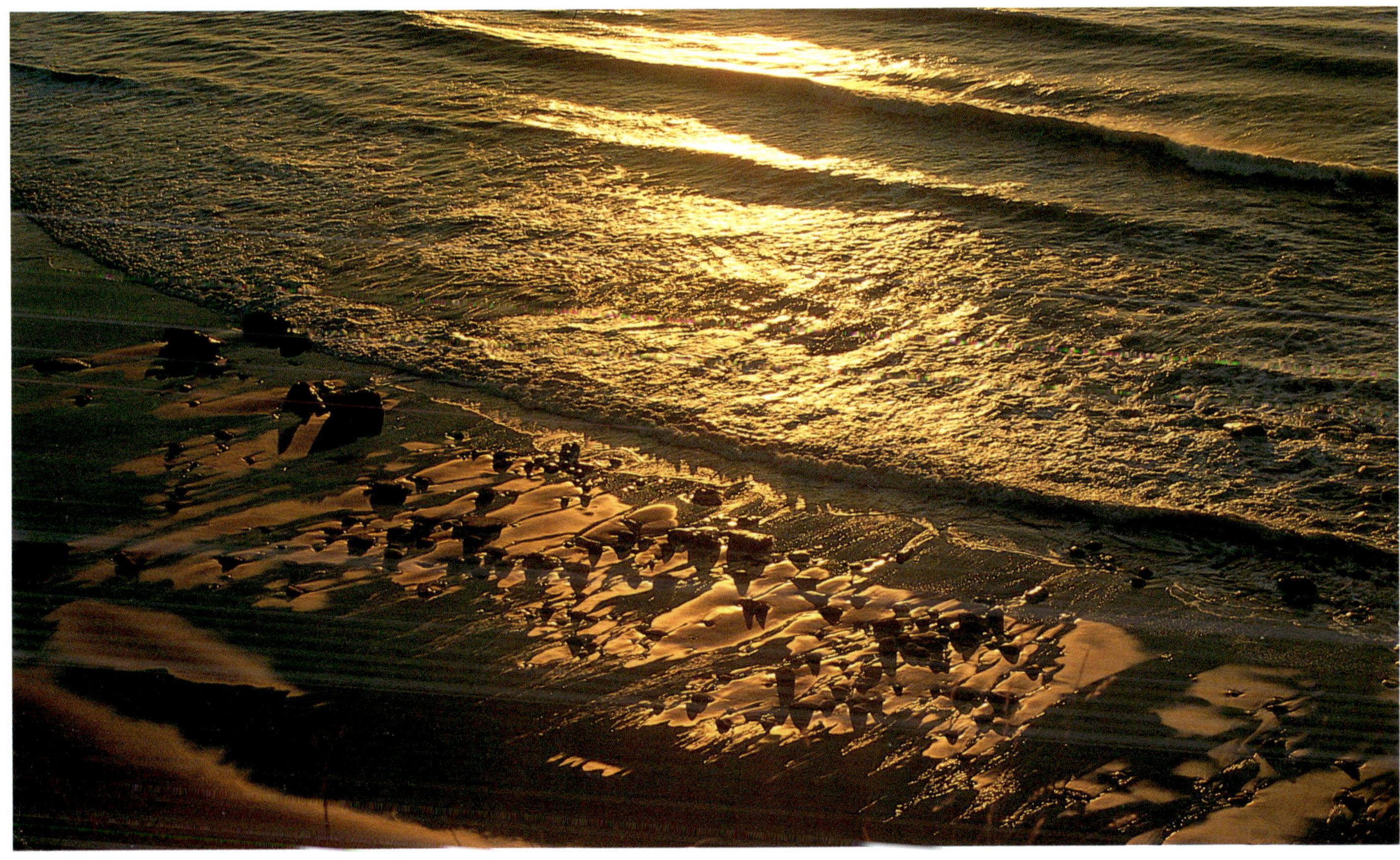

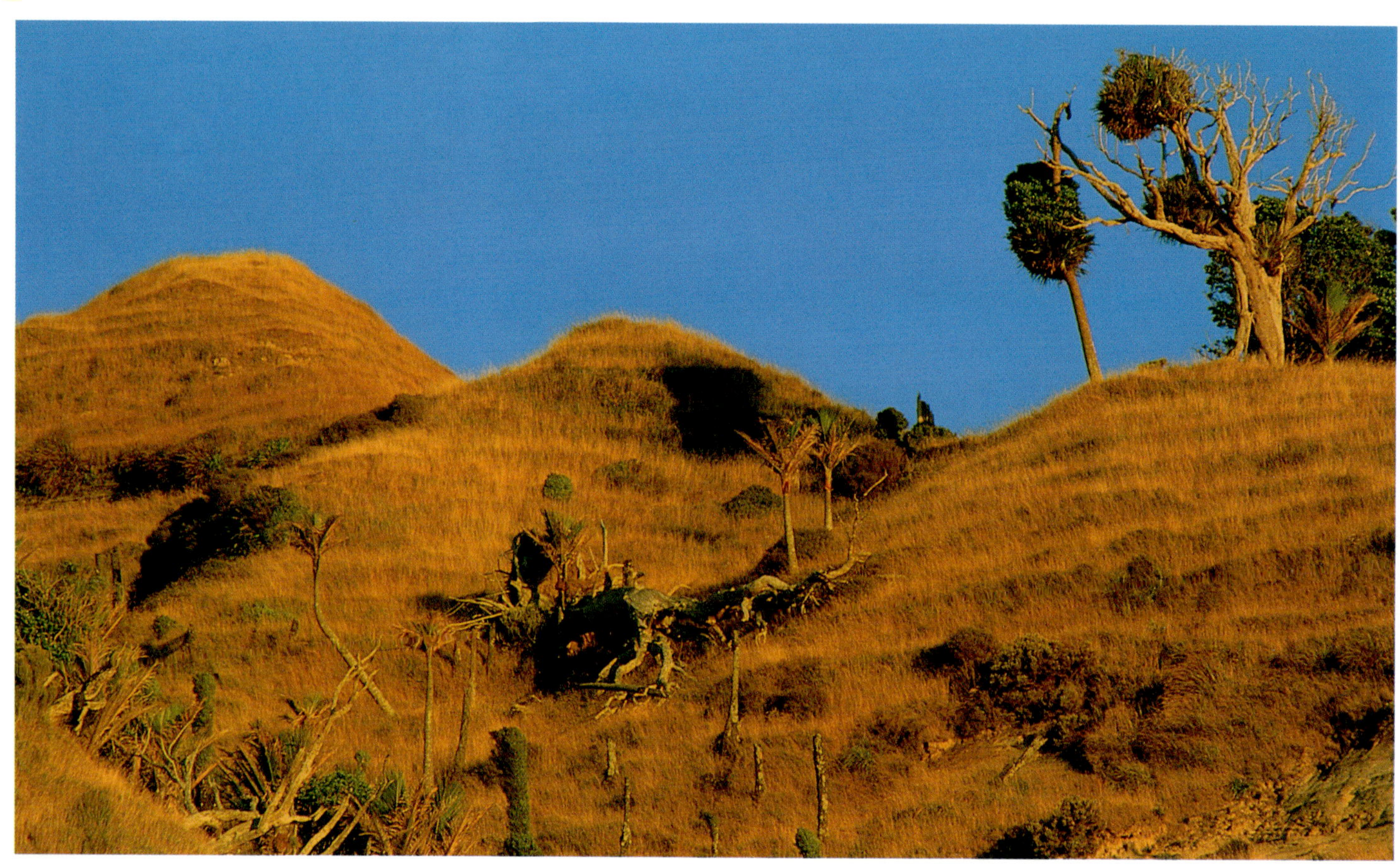

Tongaporutu

The Tongaporutu cliffs look almost Mediterranean in the last light. The blue of the sky and the rust of the burnt summer grass fascinated me. Was I really on the coast of New Zealand, or transported to the Greek Islands? The karaka tree reminds me that this really is a New Zealand scene.

Taranaki Bight

The wind and sea have shaped the Taranaki Bight. The layers of rock formed over the years tell the story of our coast. How many storms has it taken to make the holes in the rocks? How many birds have made their homes and had babies on the rock shelf? How many dads have taken their kids fishing here? Thank goodness mine did.

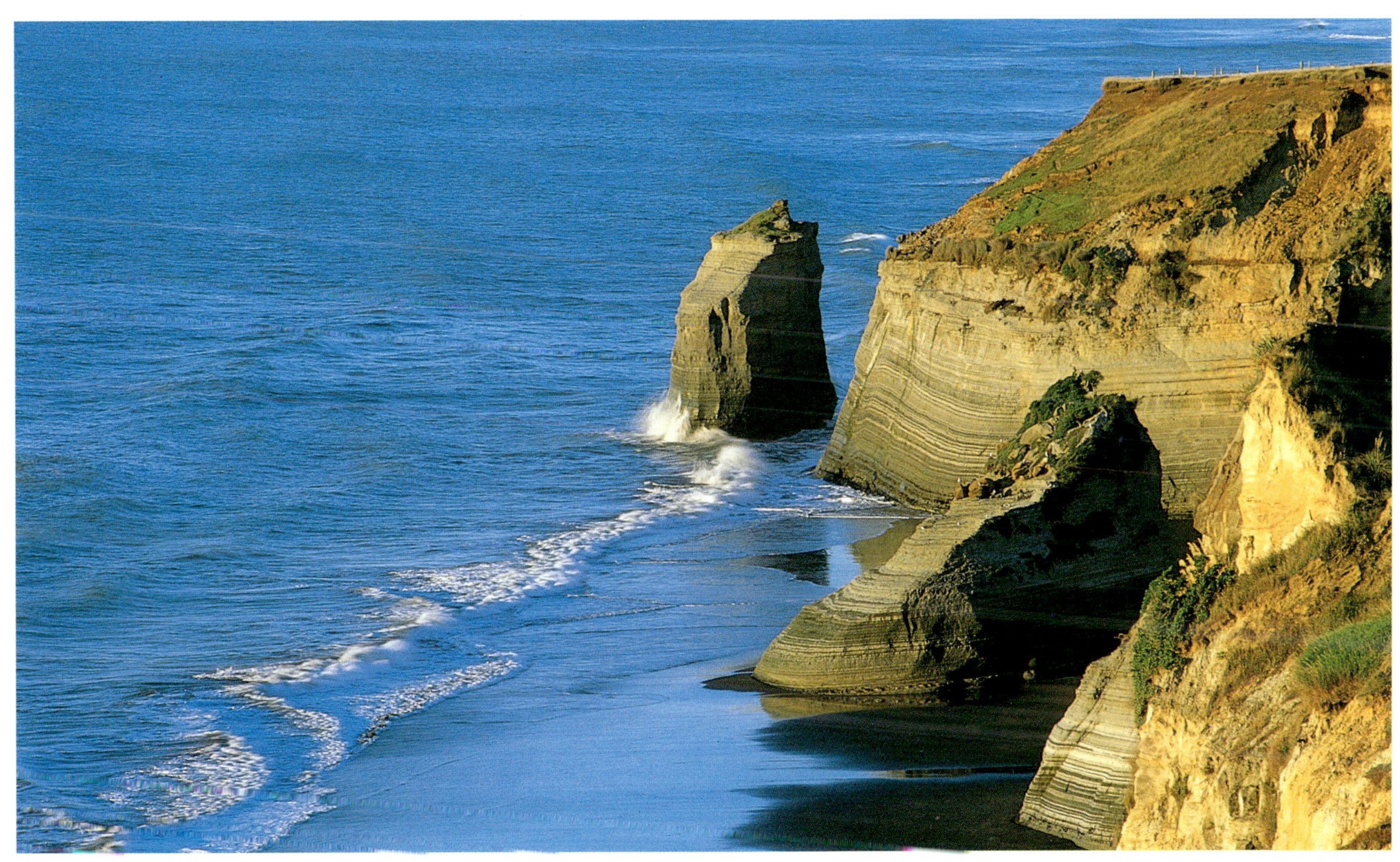

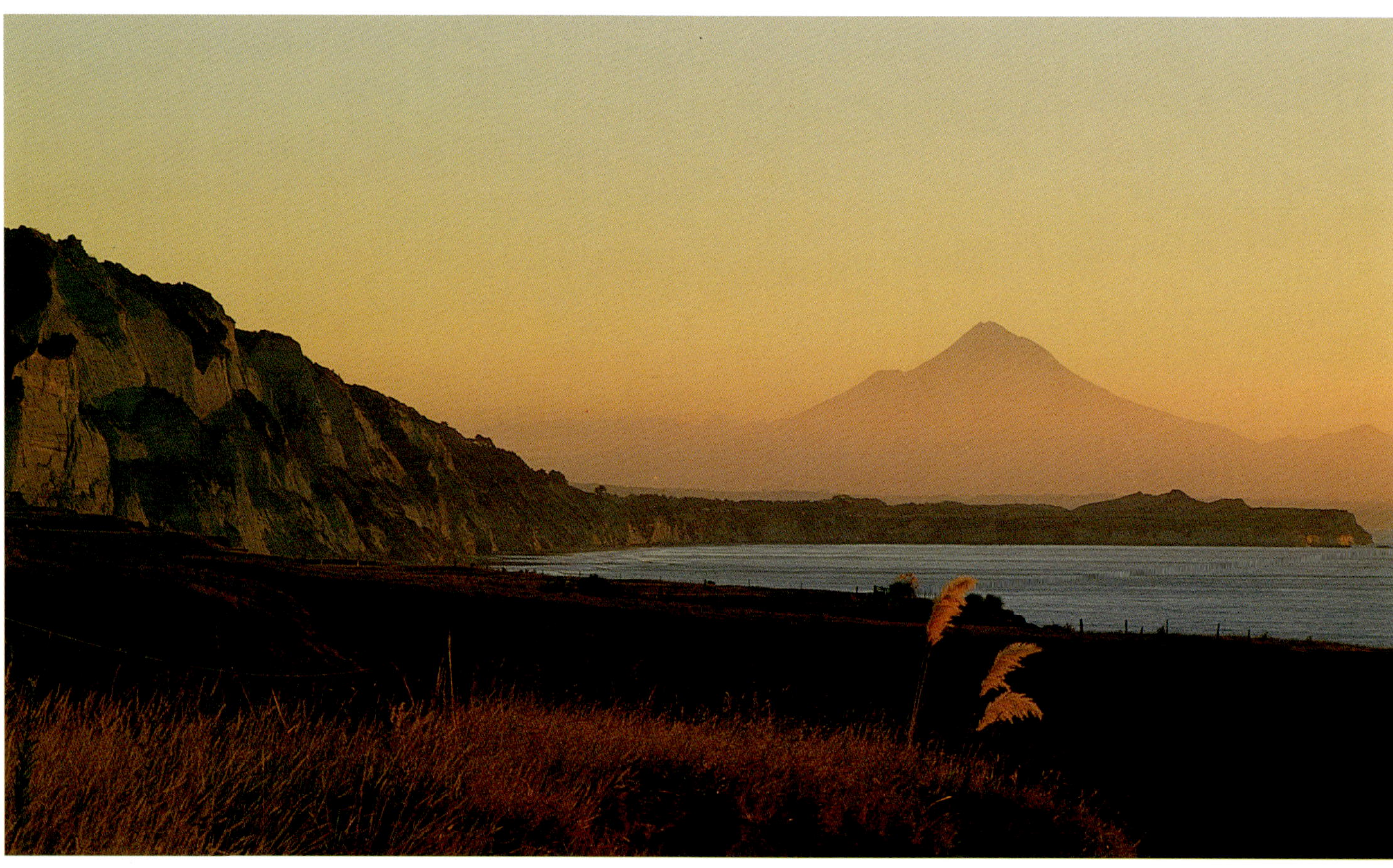

Pukearuhe

The mountain that lives by the sea. The ocean, Mount Taranaki and Pukearuhe (Whitecliffs) are a unique combination, accessible to most people in this region within 30 minutes. For those of us born in the lee of this mountain, our days and nights are influenced by its moods. We gasp at its beauty, scold it for the weather and bless it on clear days. When it's blue we wait for the snow and when it comes we dream of summer.

Uruti

Ah, the mystery of the Uruti Valley where some of the scenes from that wonderful film *The Piano* were shot. I have driven the road zillions of times on the trip to Auckland and marvelled at the way mist and frost changes the landscape. Spider webs sparkle and shape the trees.

My mother would love this and so do I.

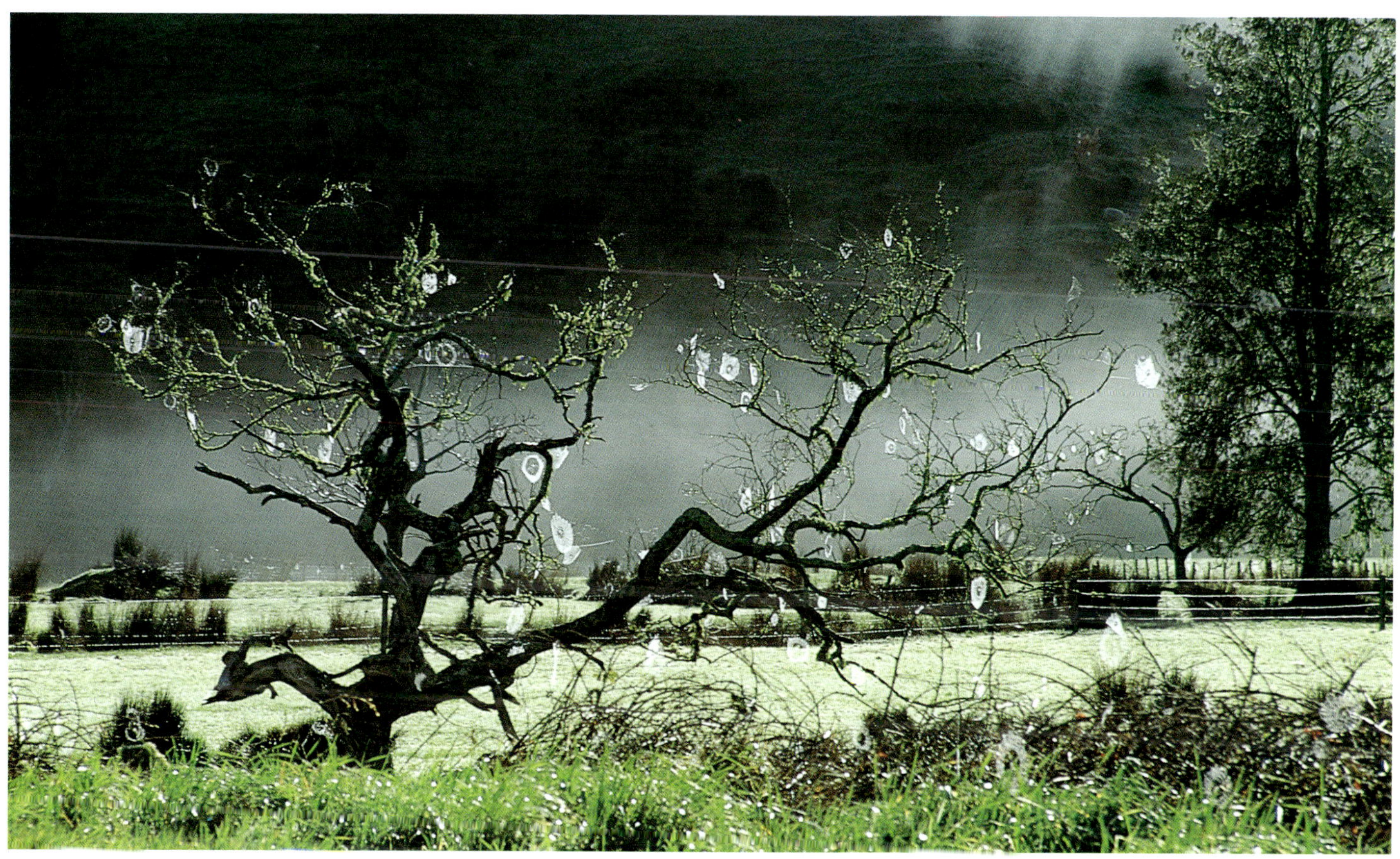

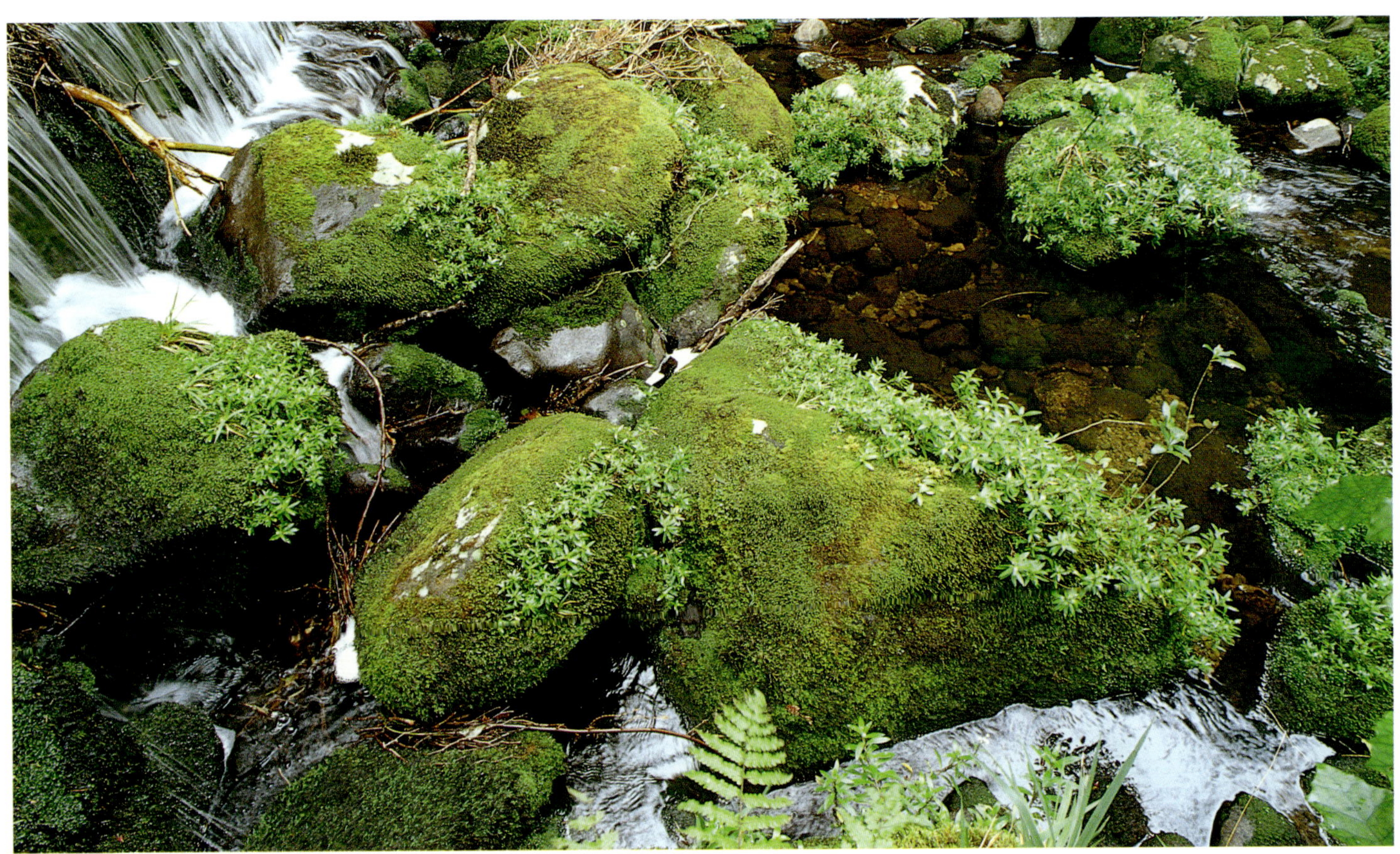

Pukeiti

The Pukeiti Rhododendron Trust gardens nestle in the hills above our farm. Like many of our streams, this one has moss and ferns growing in the shade of the bush. This stream runs through the water wheel in these internationally famous gardens.

Omata

The green of the dairy land in New Plymouth blends with the sea. Often as I drive home I marvel at its shape and colour.

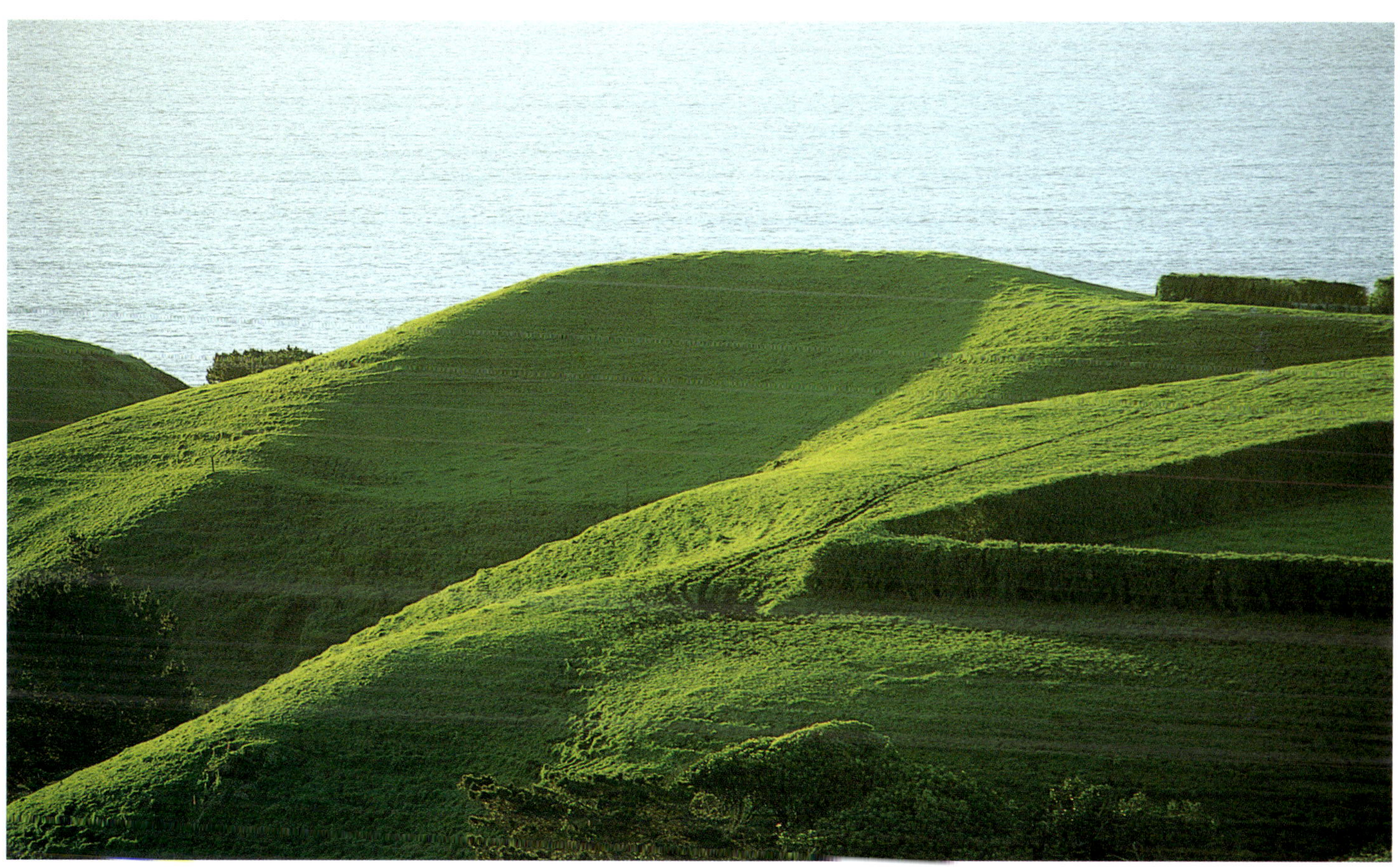

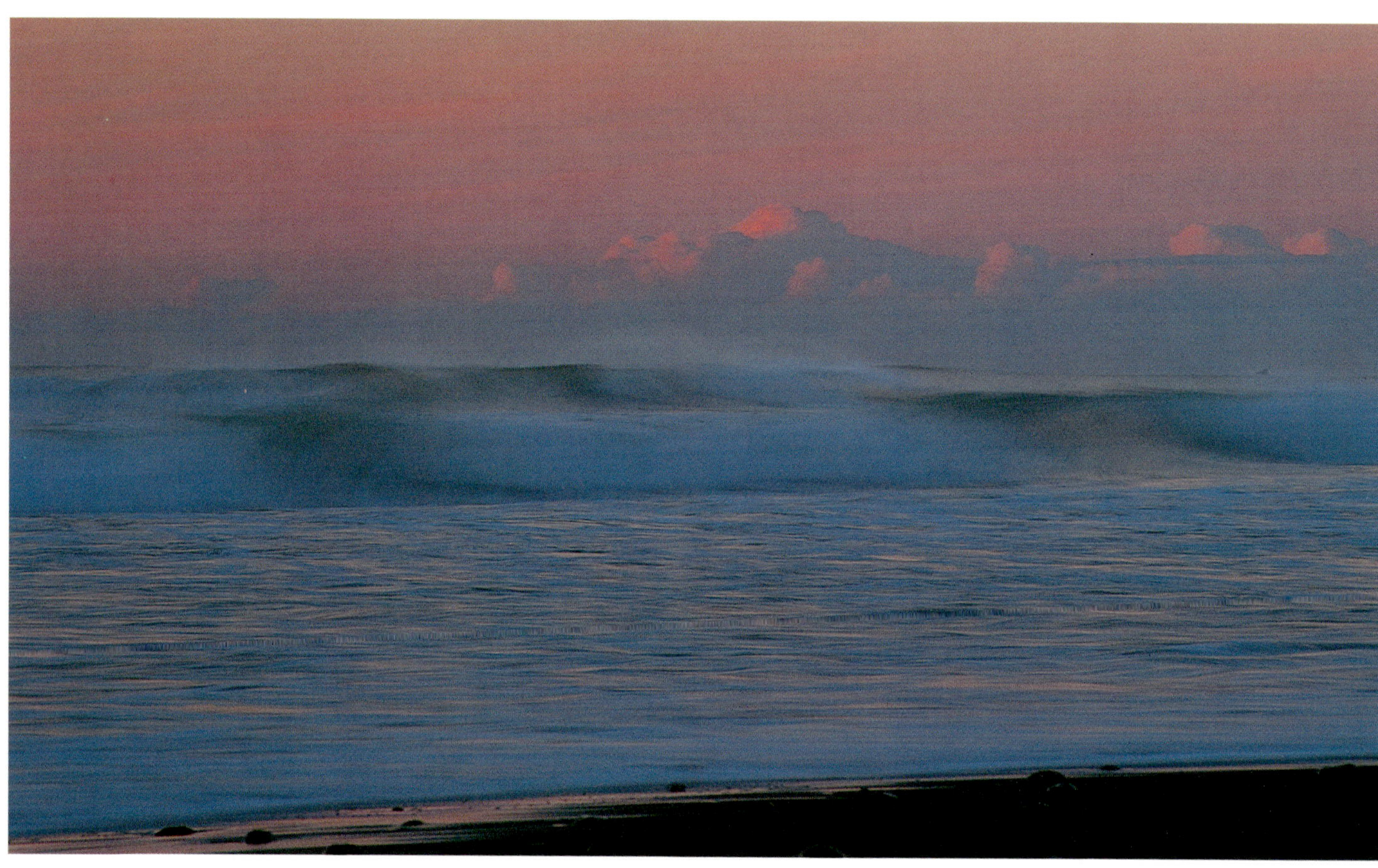

Surf Highway

Watching my son and daughter surfing for years in spots such as this has challenged me to catch water in different ways. Waves softened by the slow shutter speed seem more powerful at this my most favourite place in the world. Tide, wind and light change familiar places into exotic locations. The Oakura sunset once again turns pink and luscious.

Sugar Loaf Islands

Looking back to the Sugar Loaf Islands in New Plymouth after collecting mussels one night on a spring tide. These glorious colours started to happen after sunset and I crouched low in the water to capture them.

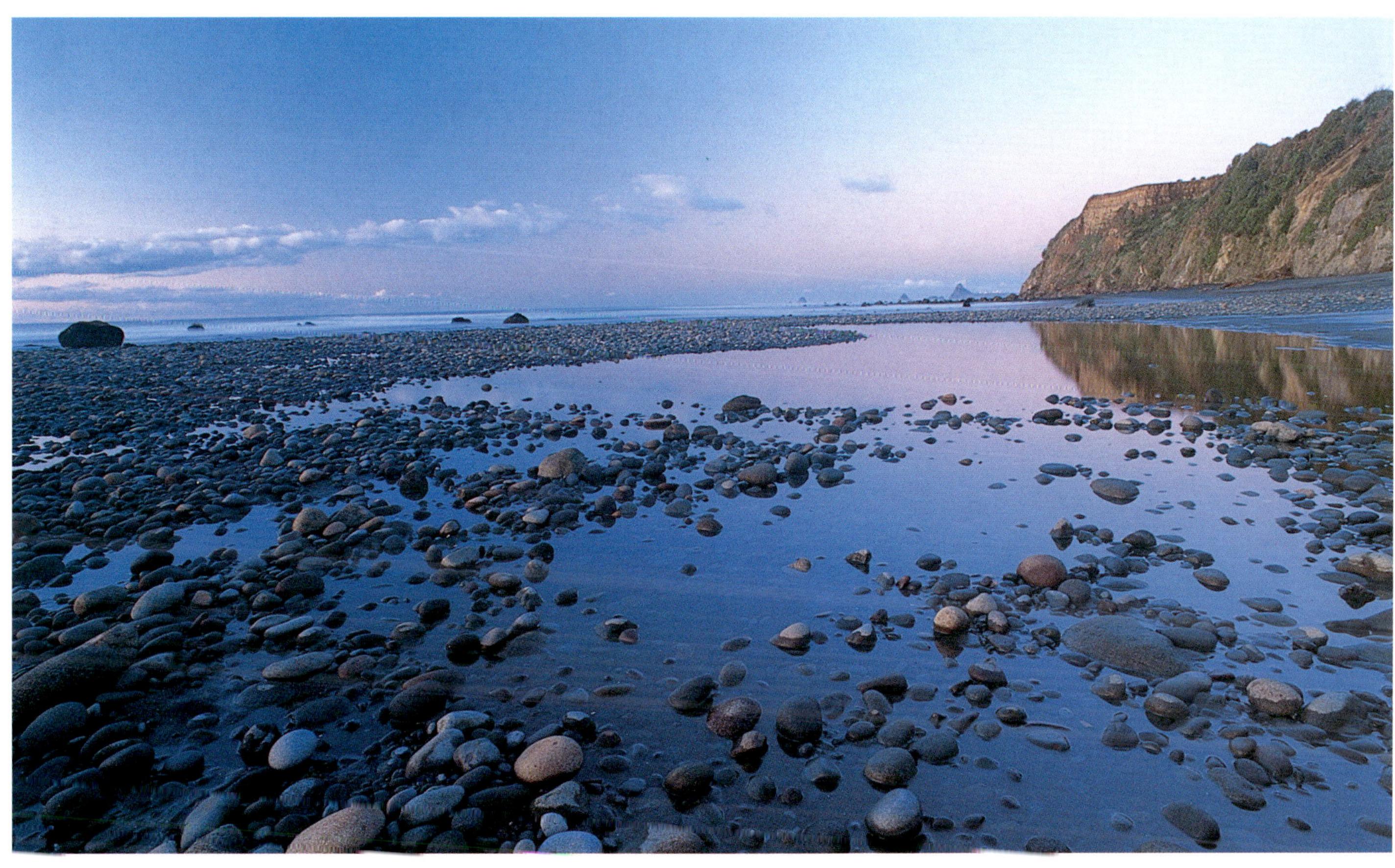

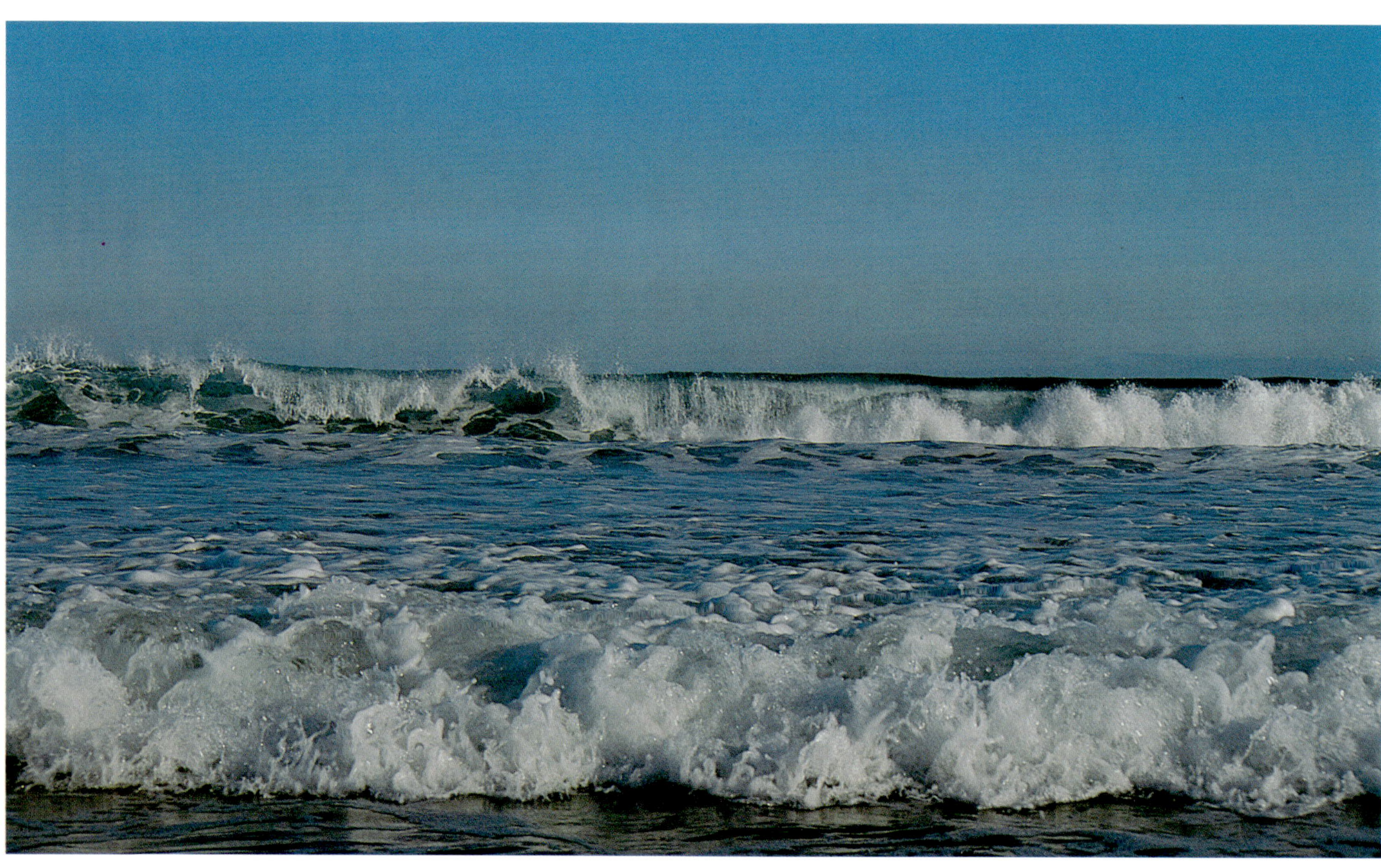

Oakura Beach

In the early morning light you can feel the crispness of the ocean as surf breaks onto the black volcanic sand on the Oakura main beach. The summer heat warms the sand for an after swim sauna as you cuddle into it.

Oakura Matapu

Oakura. I've always understood that the name is linked to the colour of the setting sun. Other interpretations are a young boy travelling across the rocks whose feet became very red, and the one I like is the laying of a red cloak on the water. Whichever is true, there is no doubt that Oakura is where "the sun lingers".

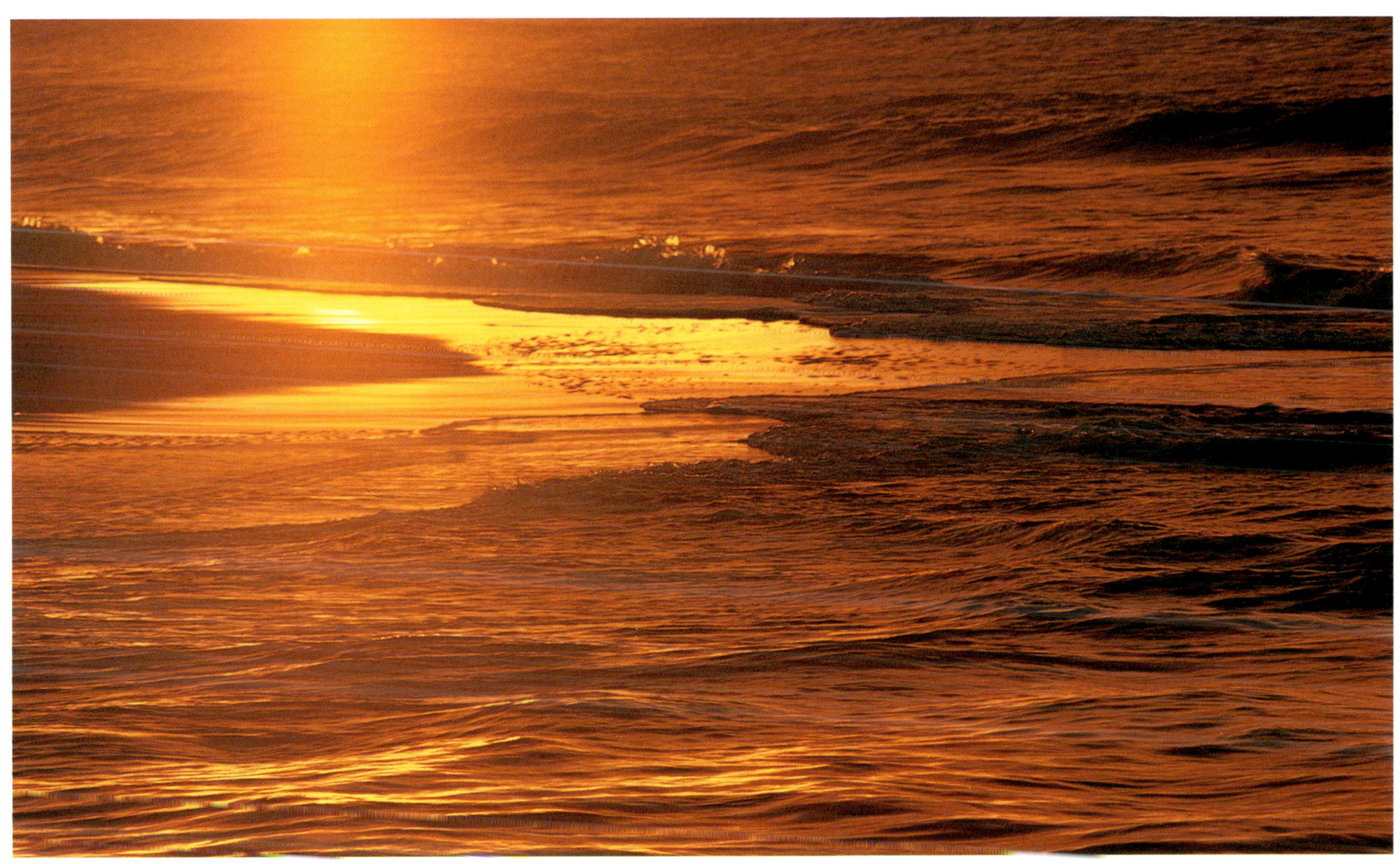

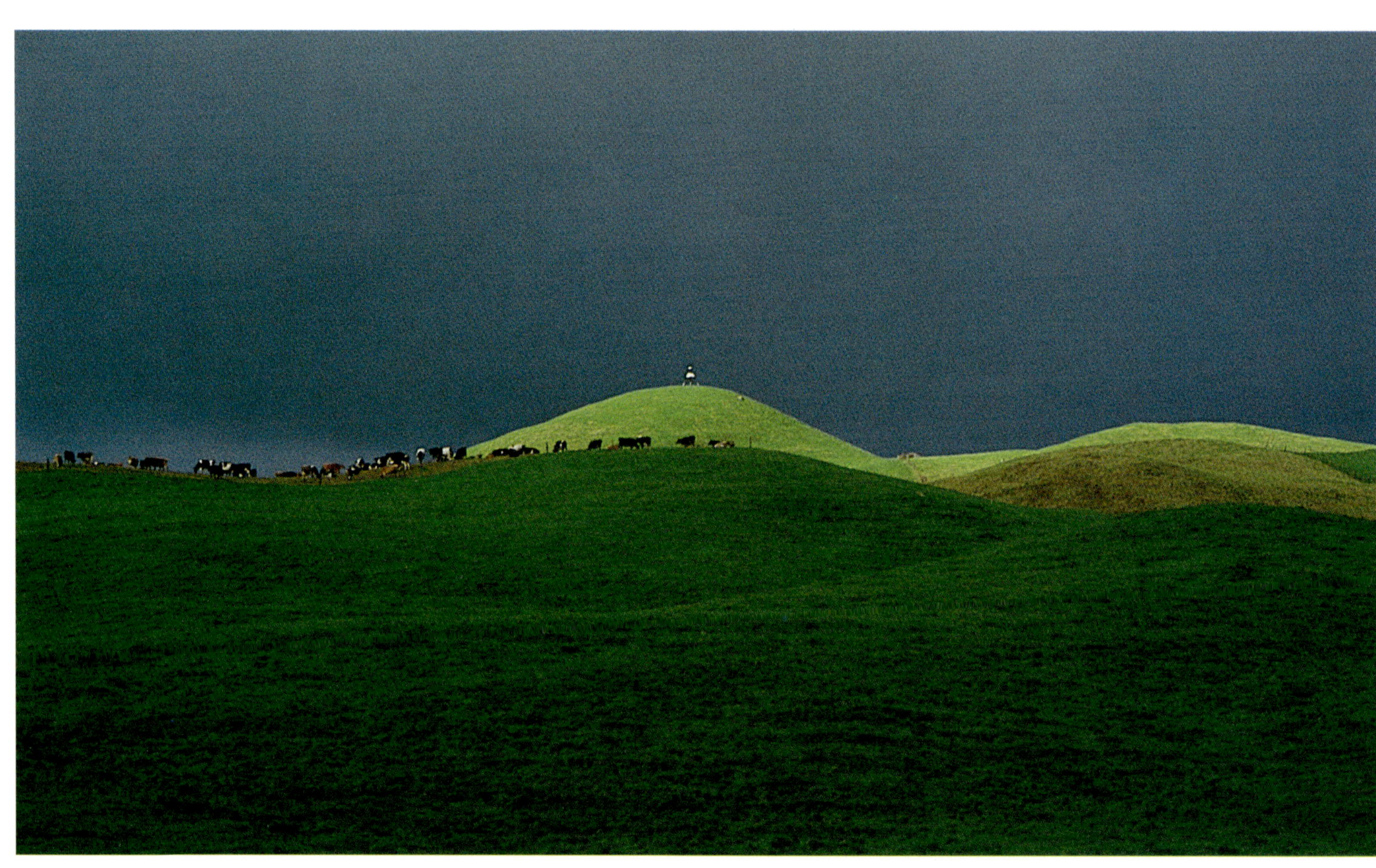

Okato

The black skies and green hills of Okato on a rainy day. The Newall Road school, which I often passed riding my horse to Bannisters, is nearby. The shaft of light is typical of the changes nature makes in the heavy clouds that gather in the Puakai Ranges and move around Mount Taranaki. This side of the mountain is where the main lava outpouring flowed to the sea, and these bumps in the landscape make the topography of this area unusual.

Dawson Falls

The snow-laden trees create an imaginary land where snowmen live. This is a children's playground and so accessible to everyone who lives in Taranaki. Our dad was a park ranger and I learned to love the bush at an early age. My sisters used to ride in a cart pulled by Chinook, our Saint Bernard dog.

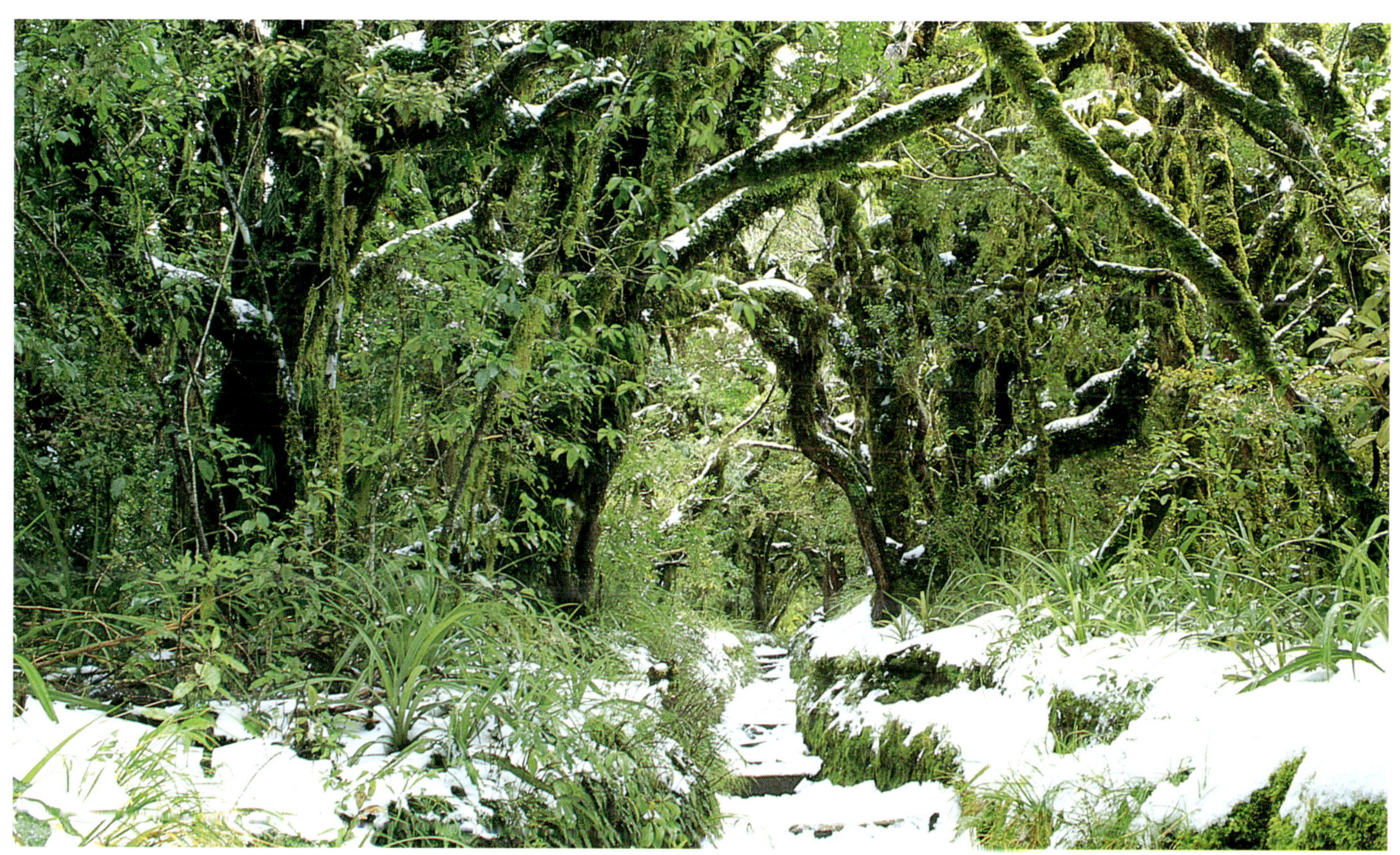

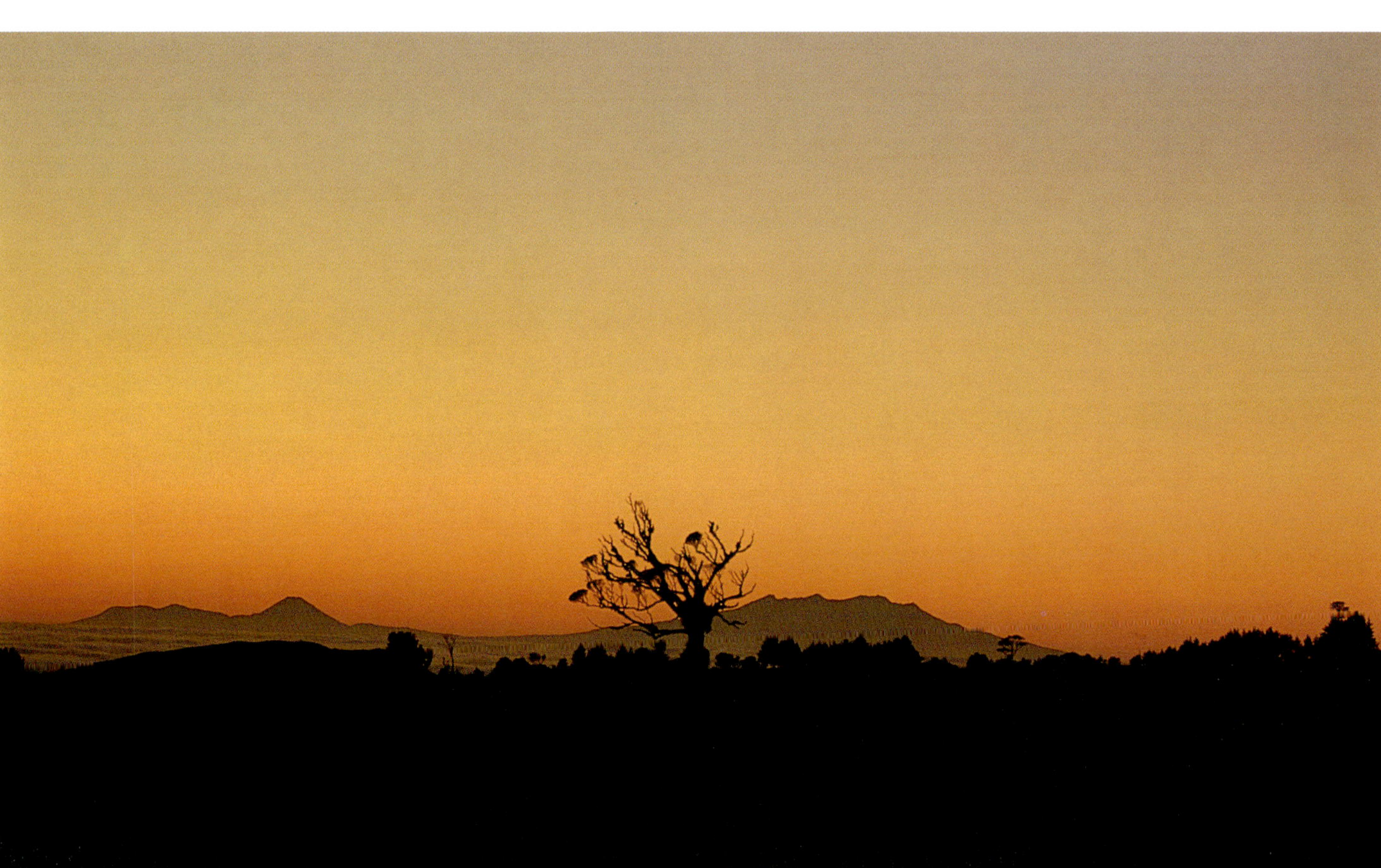

Carrington Road

An apricot dawn on Carrington Road. The distant shapes of Ruapehu, Tongariro and Ngauruhoe always remind me of the wonderful story of Mount Taranaki being cast from this distant range in a lovers' tiff. As it made its way to its present sight Mount Taranaki created the Whanganui River in its path. I wonder if the mountains can talk from this distance. I would like to think so.

Mount Taranaki

"Oh you mountain, you mighty mountain," my mother often said as we returned home. Driving north to Taranaki in the early morning, the mountain is your guide on a clear day. This was a great day – the toi toi framed Mount Taranaki just south of Patea and the ever-present wisp of cloud was perfectly placed.

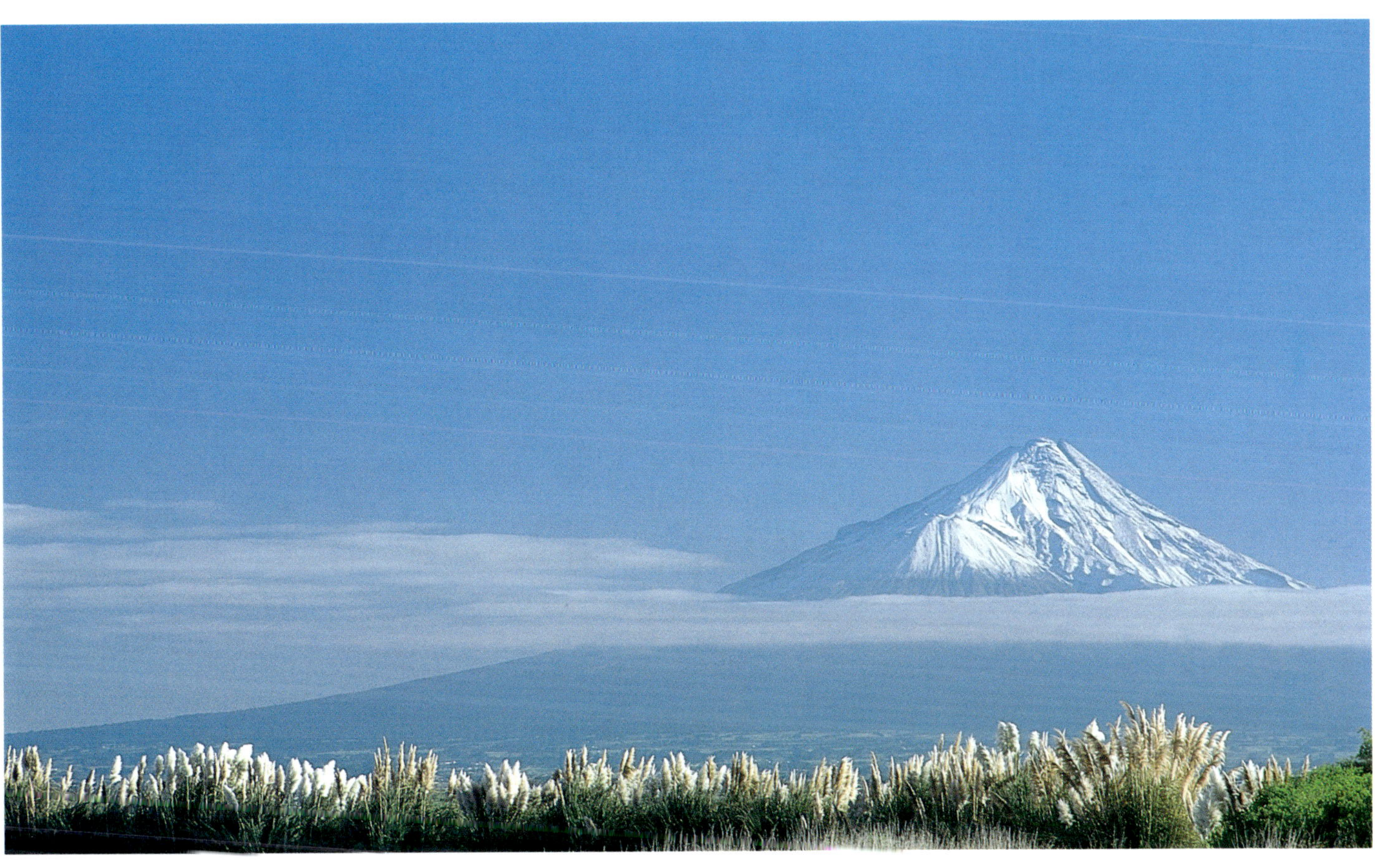

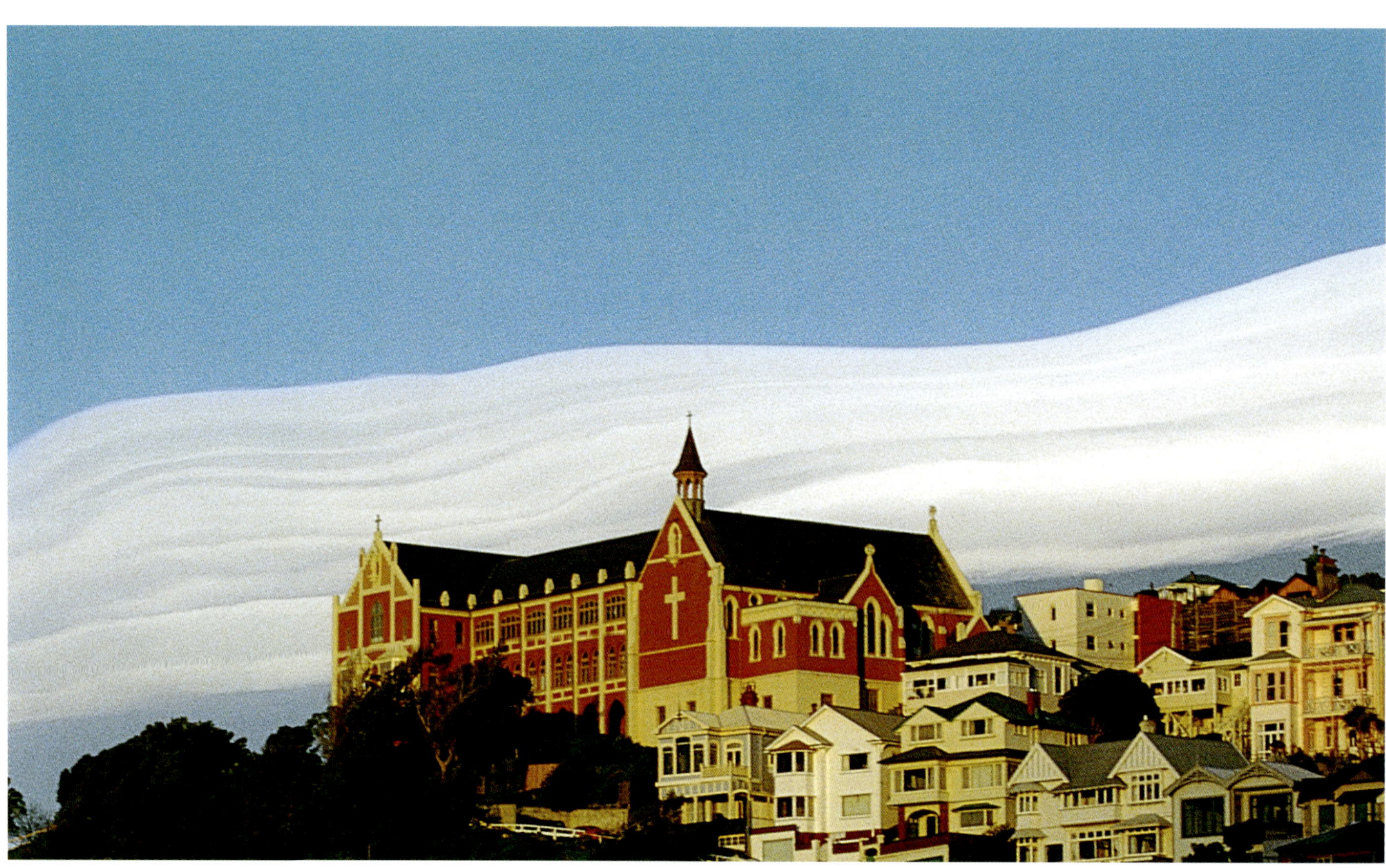

Wellington

This photo is an example of why every photographer should always carry their camera with them as an extension of their arm. I didn't have mine with me, but just had time to go and pick it up and then race back to the overseas terminal and shoot this magic snow cloud framing the hills of Wellington.

People kept coming up and asking if I would send them the shot – so here you are.

Kaikoura

I cancelled my flight from Christchurch so I could drive up the coast on this glorious day. The view didn't disappoint me as the Kaikoura coast spread out before my 20 mm lens. This is the whale-watching mecca of New Zealand.

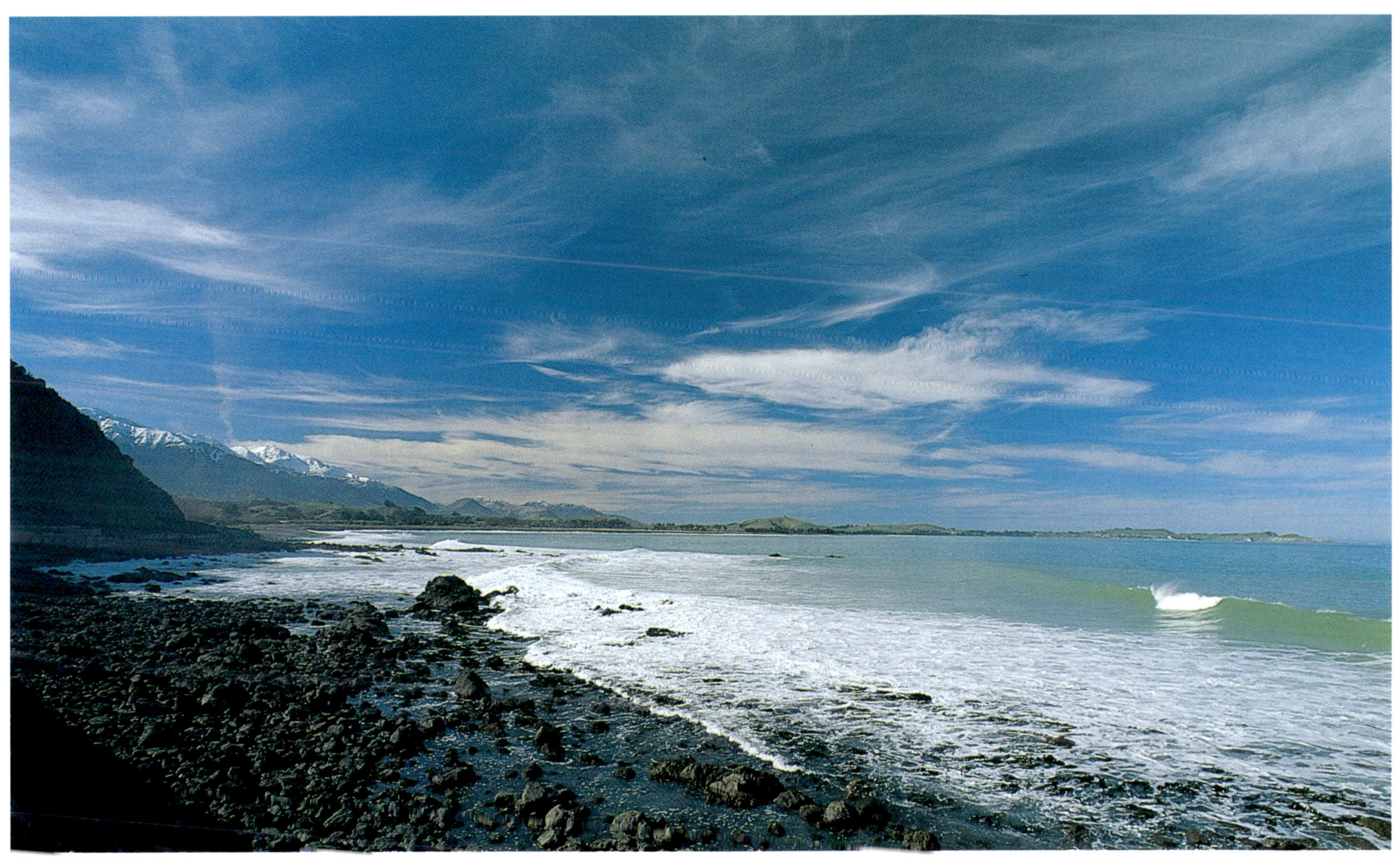

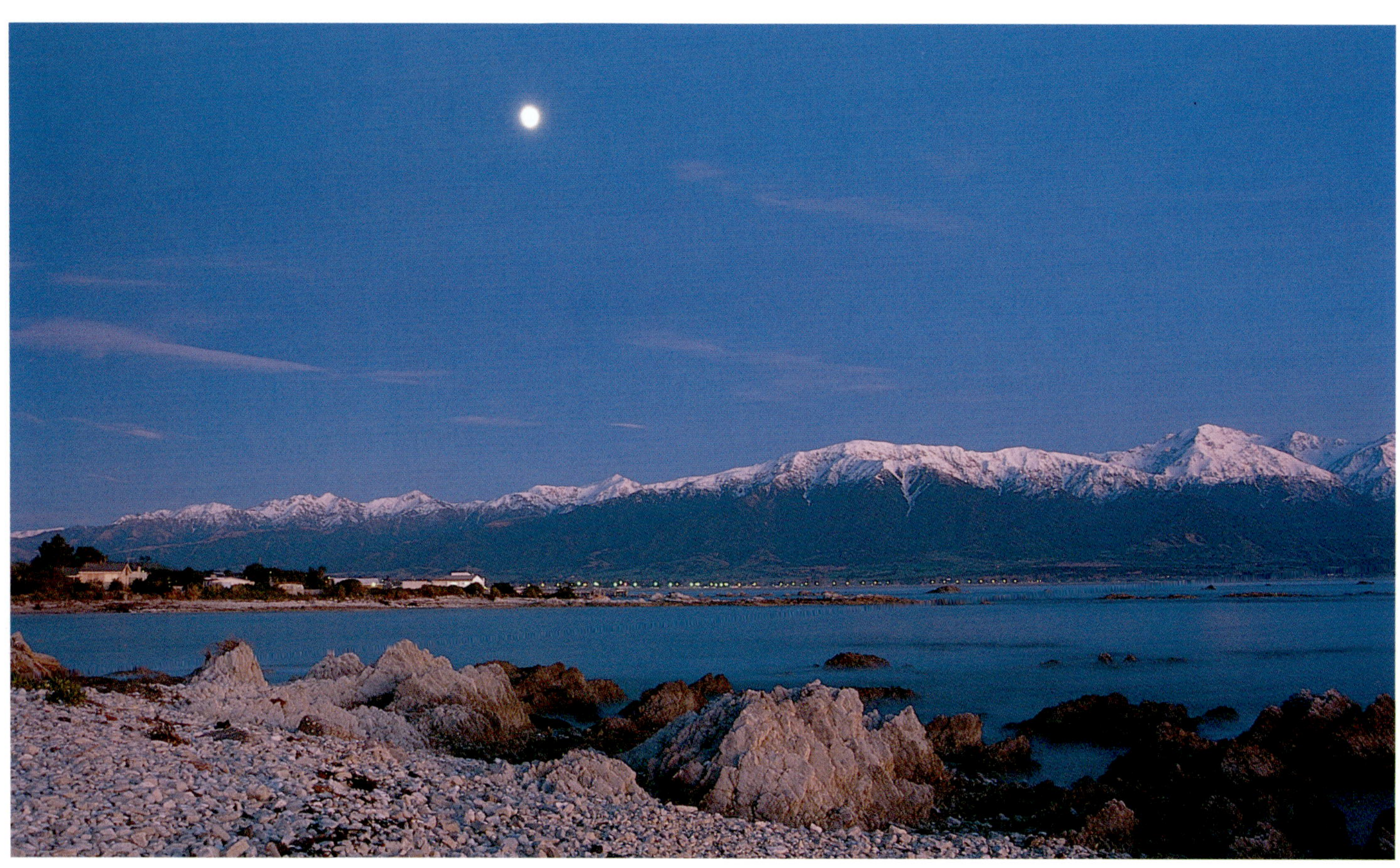

The Kaikouras

The early-morning rule really worked here. I froze as I watched in awe as the early light turned the Kaikoura Ranges mauve and cream. The slow shutter speed softened the water on the rocks and the moon seemed to hang around just to affirm my early vigil.

Akaroa Road

Once again luck was with us on the drive from Akaroa to Christchurch. Fresh snow on the Southern Alps and a perfect morning made me reach for my camera yet again. Views like this are around every corner as you approach the city.

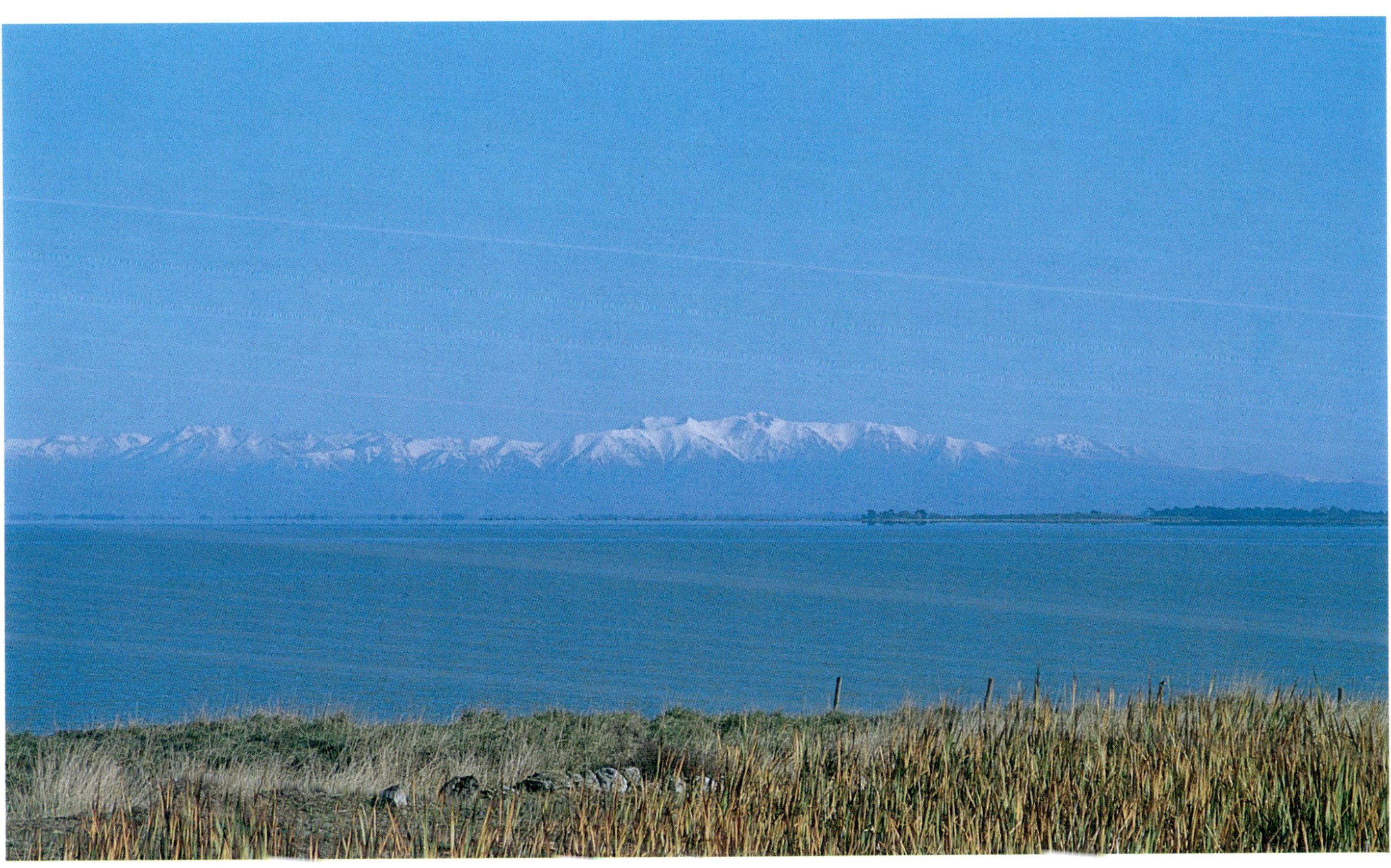

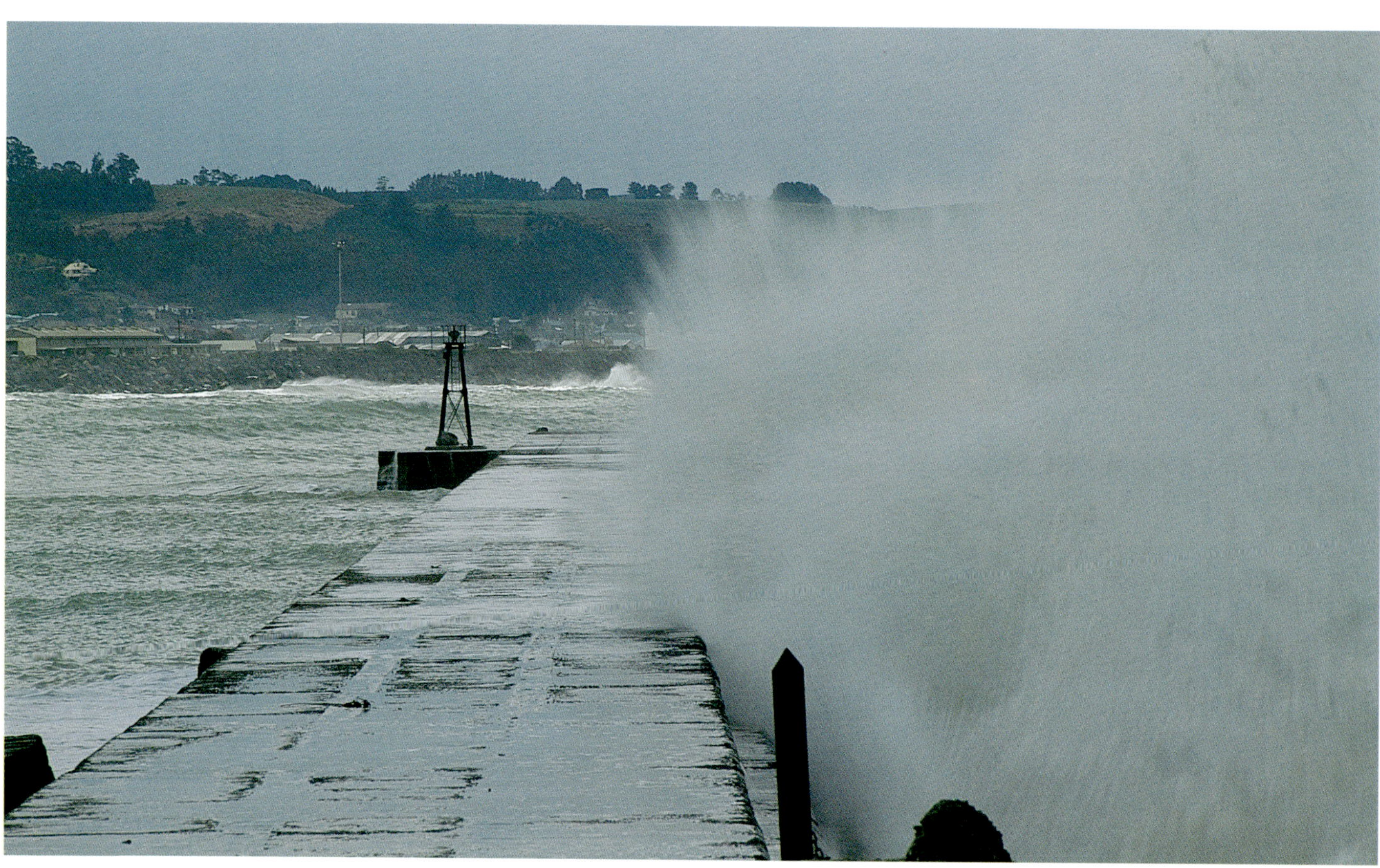

Oamaru

Although we were too early to see the blue penguins from the viewing platform at Oamaru harbour, we were entertained by the power of the Pacific Ocean as a south-easterly swell blew in and pounded the sea wall. The heritage trail through this city is great and the architecture awesome.

Moeraki

The Moeraki Boulders are a phenomenon of nature. We counted 54 of them, including the two just emerging from the cliff. Standing on the beach in the dark, watching the tide drop and the sun rise to reveal these awesome, huge rock pearls, Harry and I were completely overawed. I had goose bumps watching them through the lens. I shot three rolls of film and love every one.

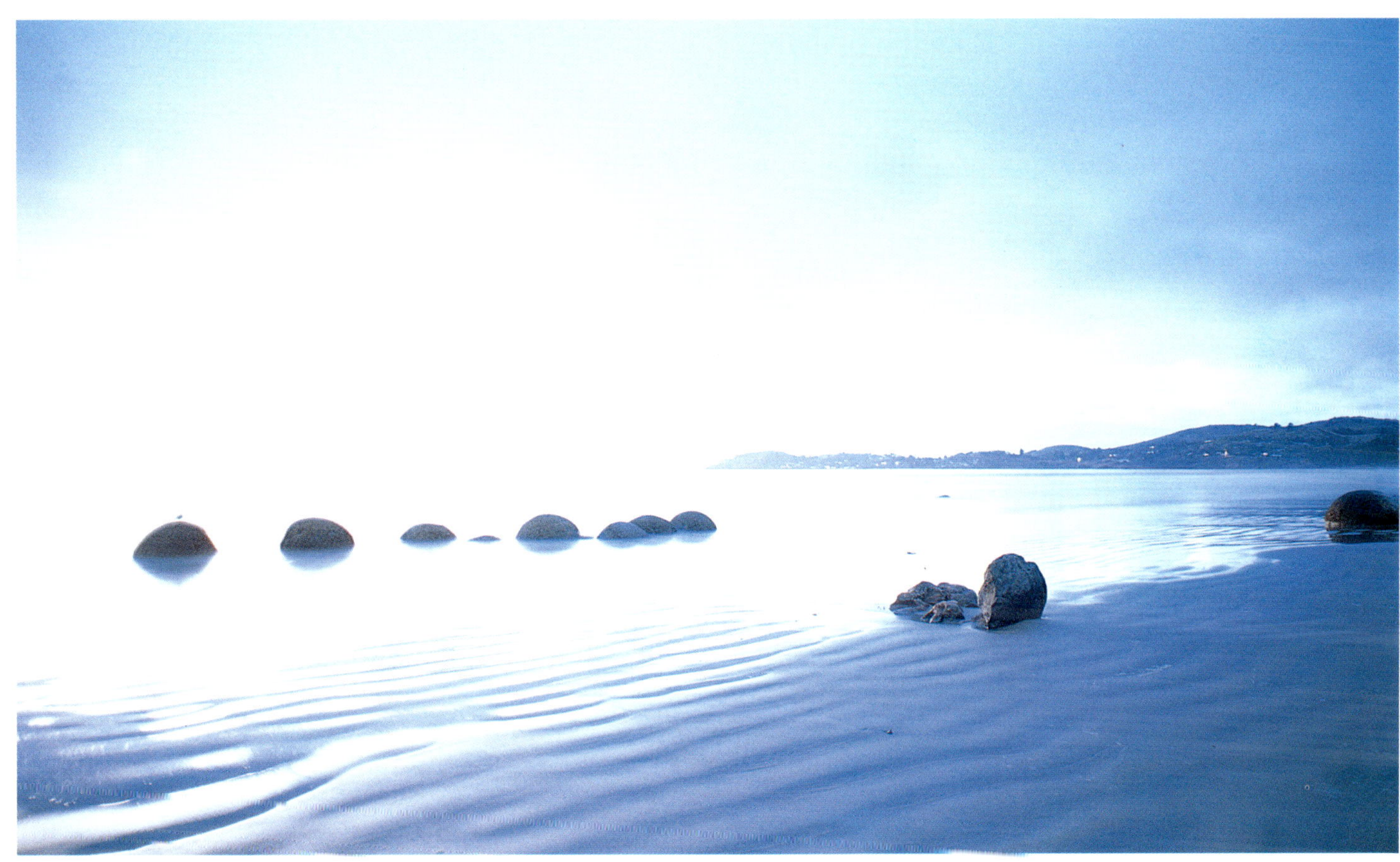

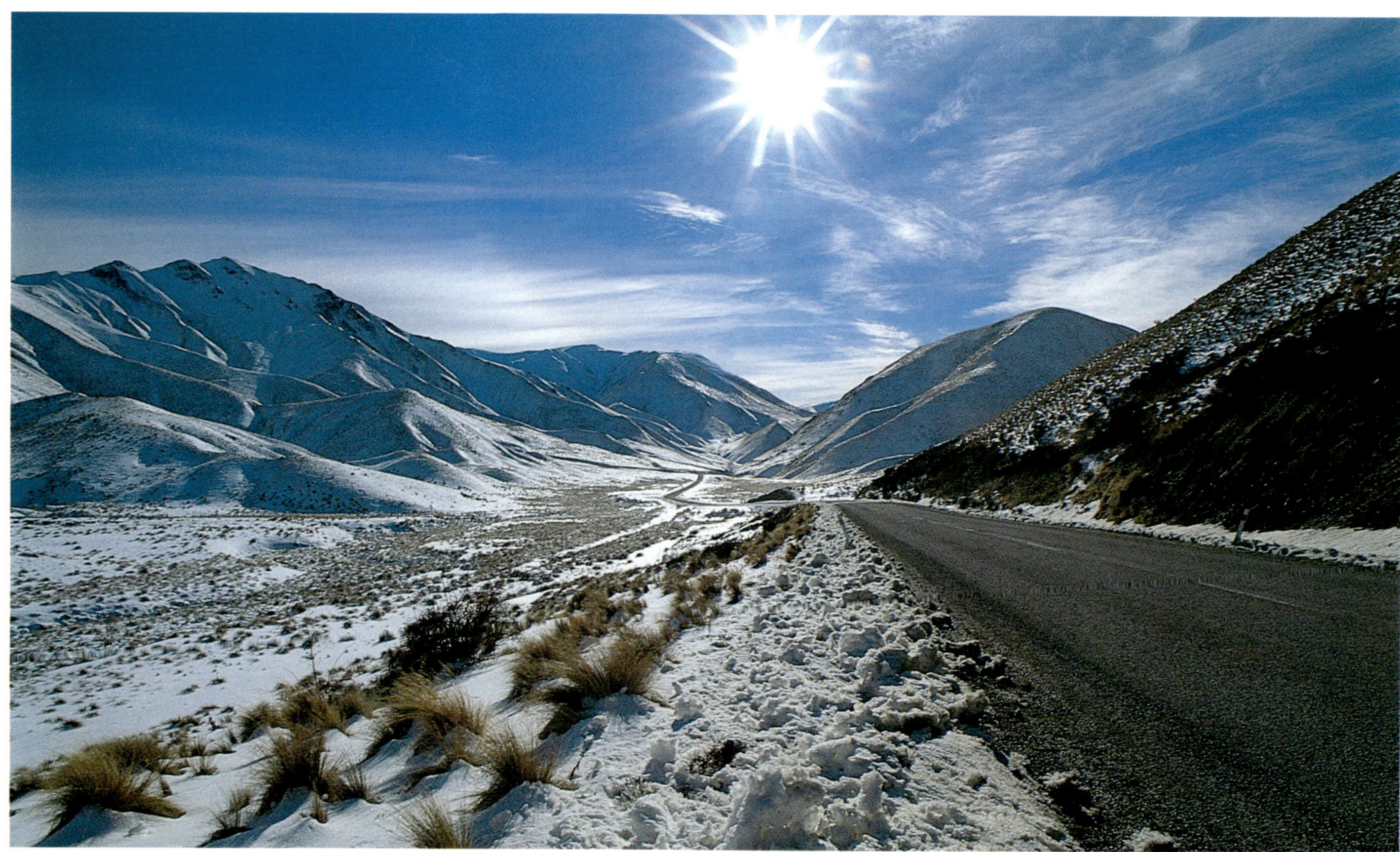

Lindis Pass, Otago

The miles we travelled in our campervan sped by and we hardly spoke as we took in the incredible beauty around us. The wall-to-wall snow that was parted only by clean, well-managed roads made this journey unforgettable. Here we are just below the summit of the Lindis Pass.

Mount Cook

Mount Cook was shrouded in cloud when we arrived and it would have been easy to miss this shot. The mountain stayed hidden for two long hours and, just as I had given up, a shimmer of light appeared through the cloud and slowly the day cleared until I had my first sight of this New Zealand icon. My patience was rewarded and Harry had a pleasant tramp in the surrounding hills while I waited.

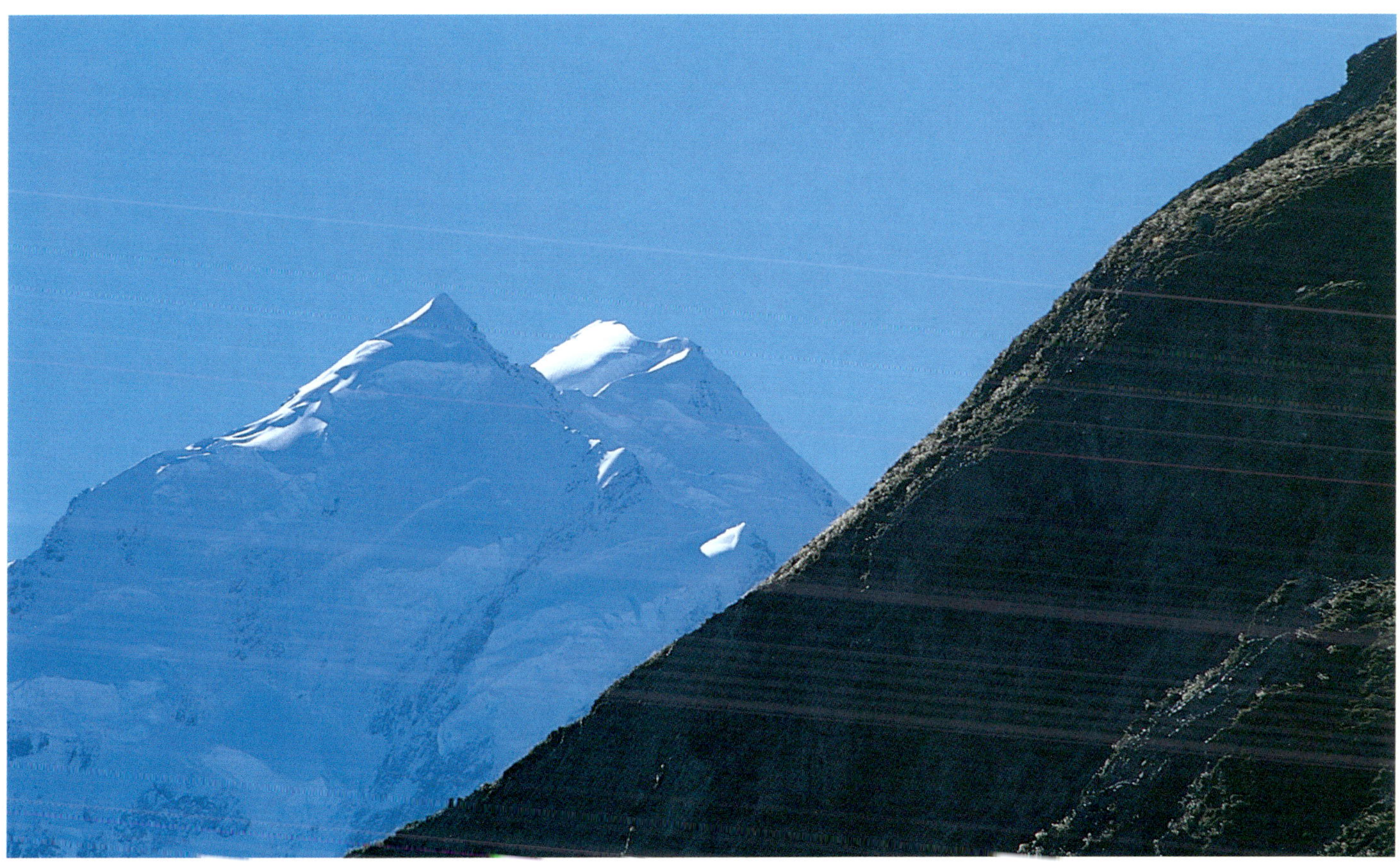

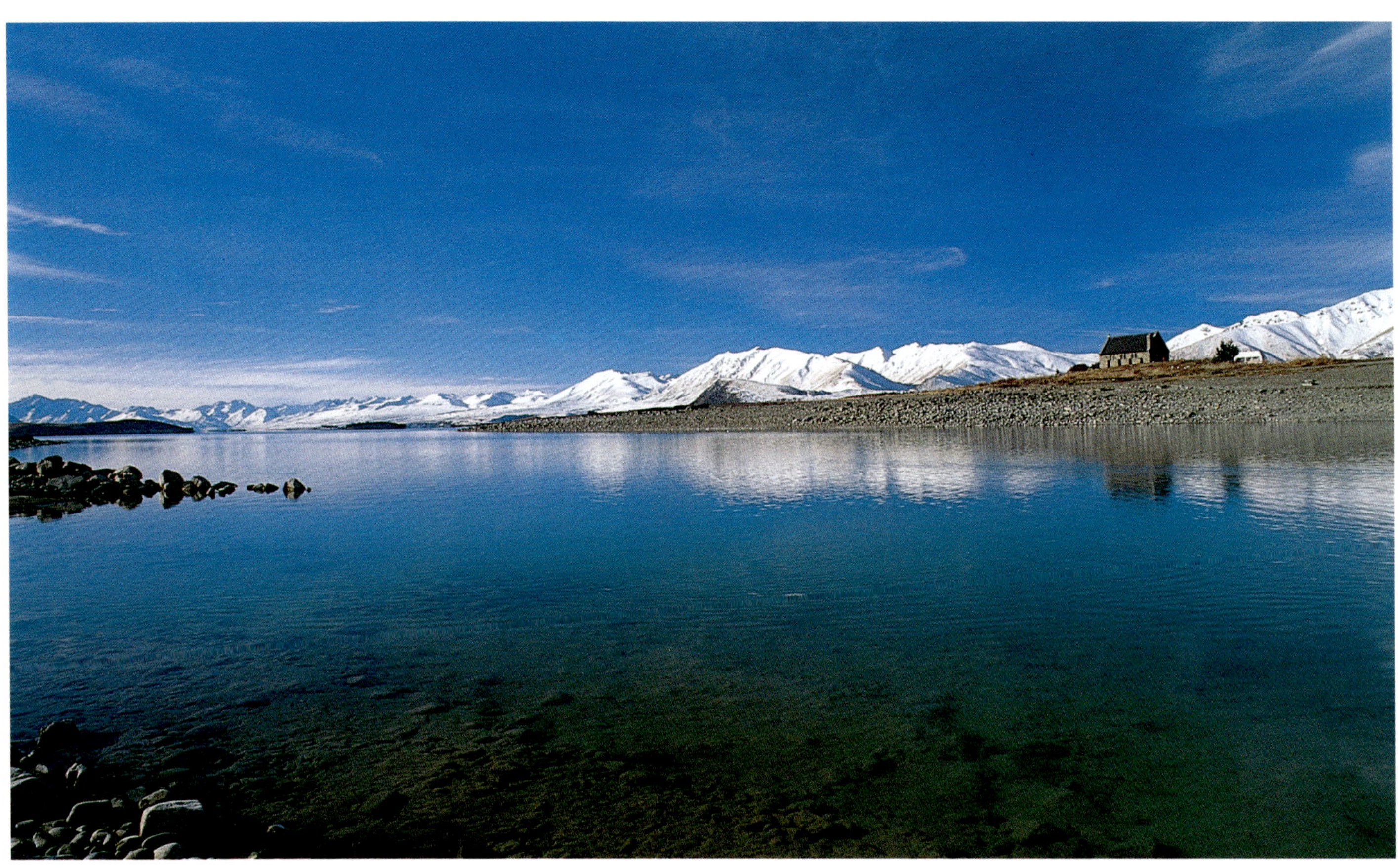

Lake Tekapo

The Church of the Good Shepherd. This is exactly what postcards are made of. My original shot was an autumn one but I was lucky enough to enjoy another view in July when snow covered the mountains – and it seemed right. Tekapo also introduced me to my first ever skating rink. It was tucked under the trees on the western side of the lake and there I watched many happy children and their parents enjoying themselves.

Haast

Haast Pass is steep and winding, dominated by mountains and rivers like this one. Sunlight on the water attracts me to this river that is so clean you want to paddle in it. Further down on the river flat we see the cattle swimming back to the unfenced plains they graze.

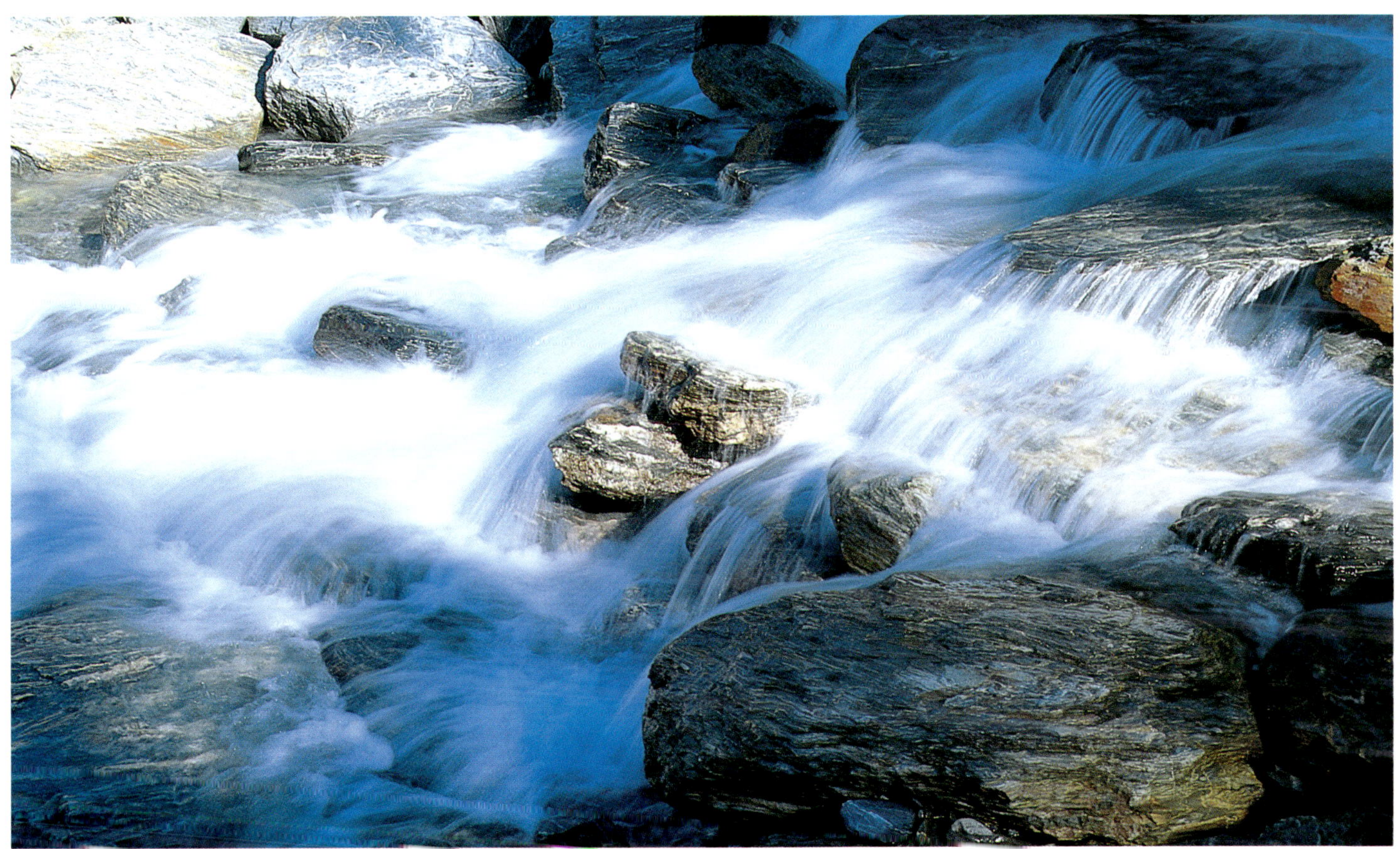

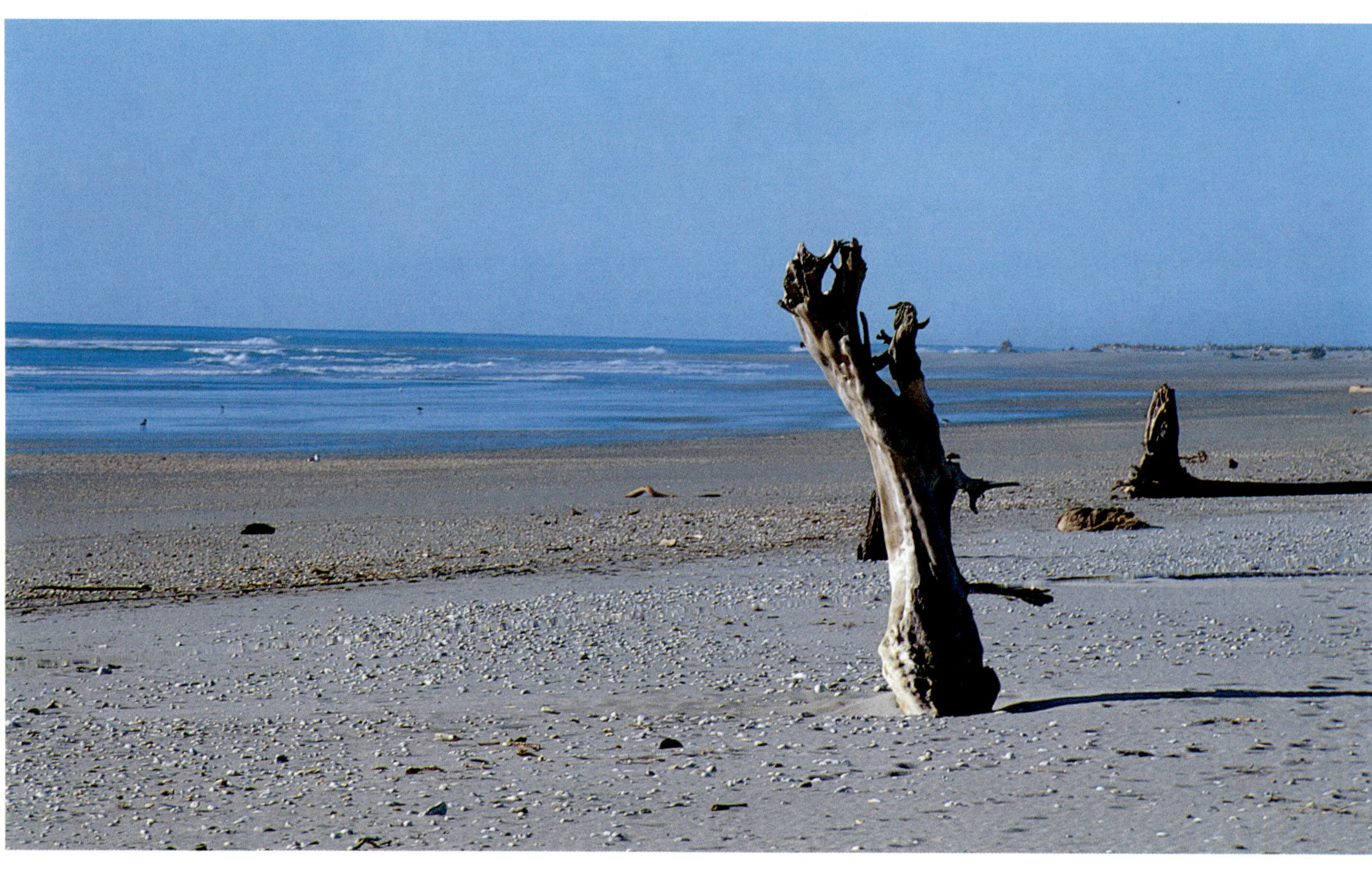

West Coast

A few days without the ocean and all Tasman Sea-watchers like me get edgy. When we arrived at Haast we headed for the ocean and a breath of salt air to recharge ourselves. Large whitebait fritters at the pub helped. Haast Beach stretches for miles and this day we saw it at its most peaceful. The hundreds of logs leave evidence of the storms which prevail here.

Cromwell

I've only been to Cromwell in autumn, but I want to go there in spring. If it's anywhere near as beautiful as this apricot orchard dappled in evening light, it will be worth the trip.

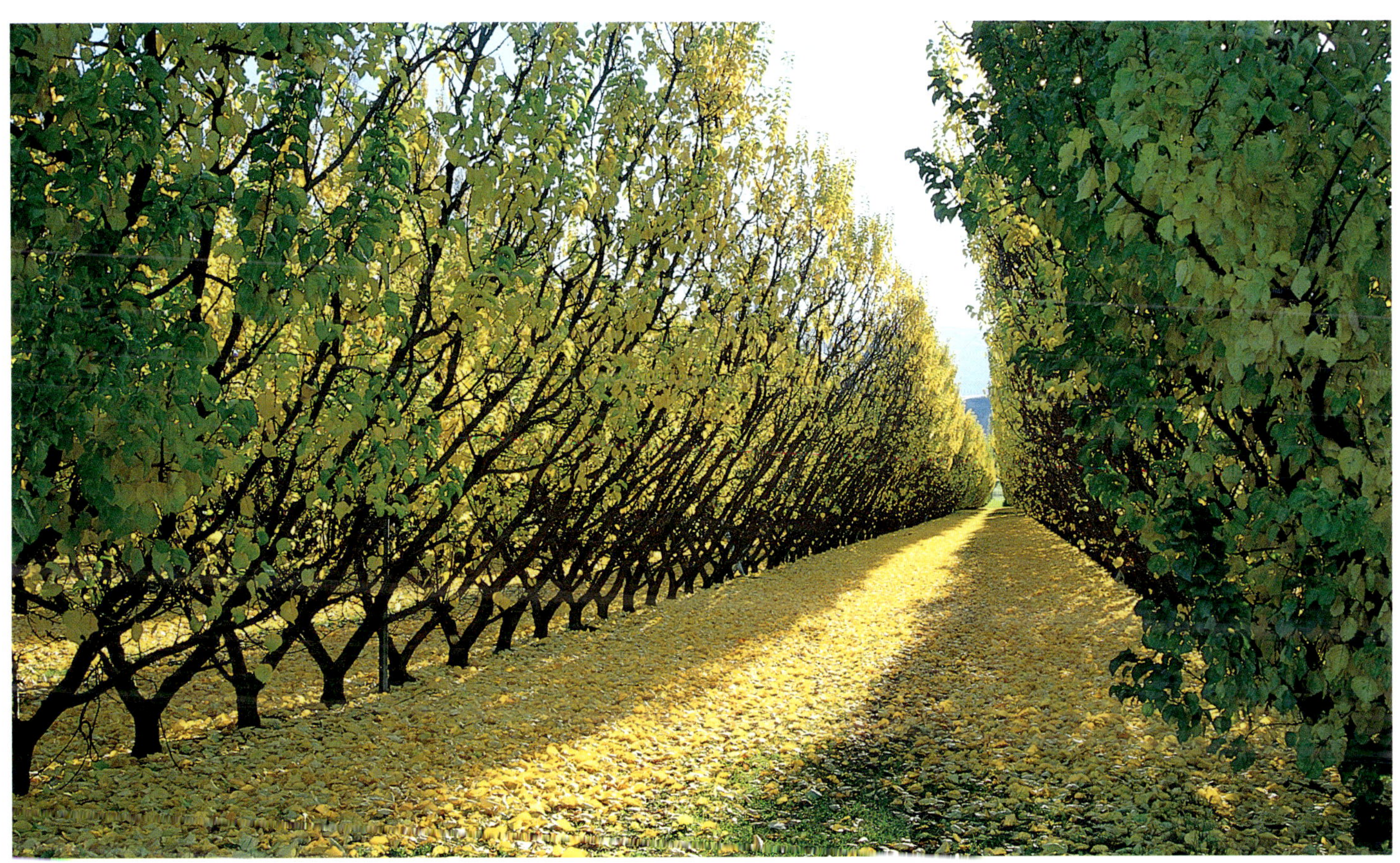

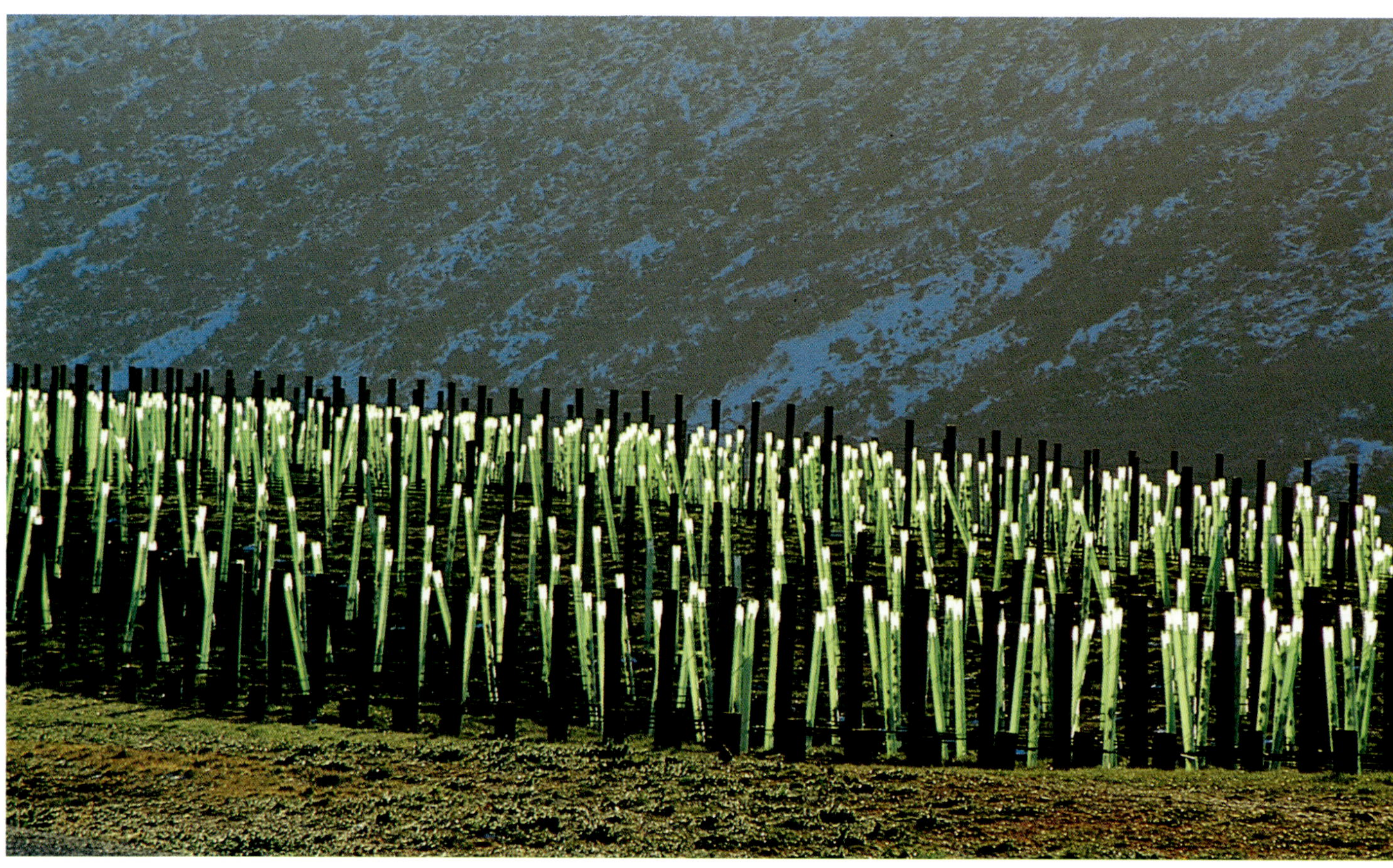

The Cromwell Road

I shot many rolls of Velvia as we travelled from Dunedin to Queenstown. As we turned a corner on the Cromwell road, the back lighting on the Peregine Vineyards made me gasp. The young vines are encased in green plastic around their bases and the effect of this is stunning in the last rays of the sun.

The Crown Range

This image shows the terraced hills above the Cromwell road. I enjoy the way the light highlights specific areas for a moment and turns the land into graphic shapes.

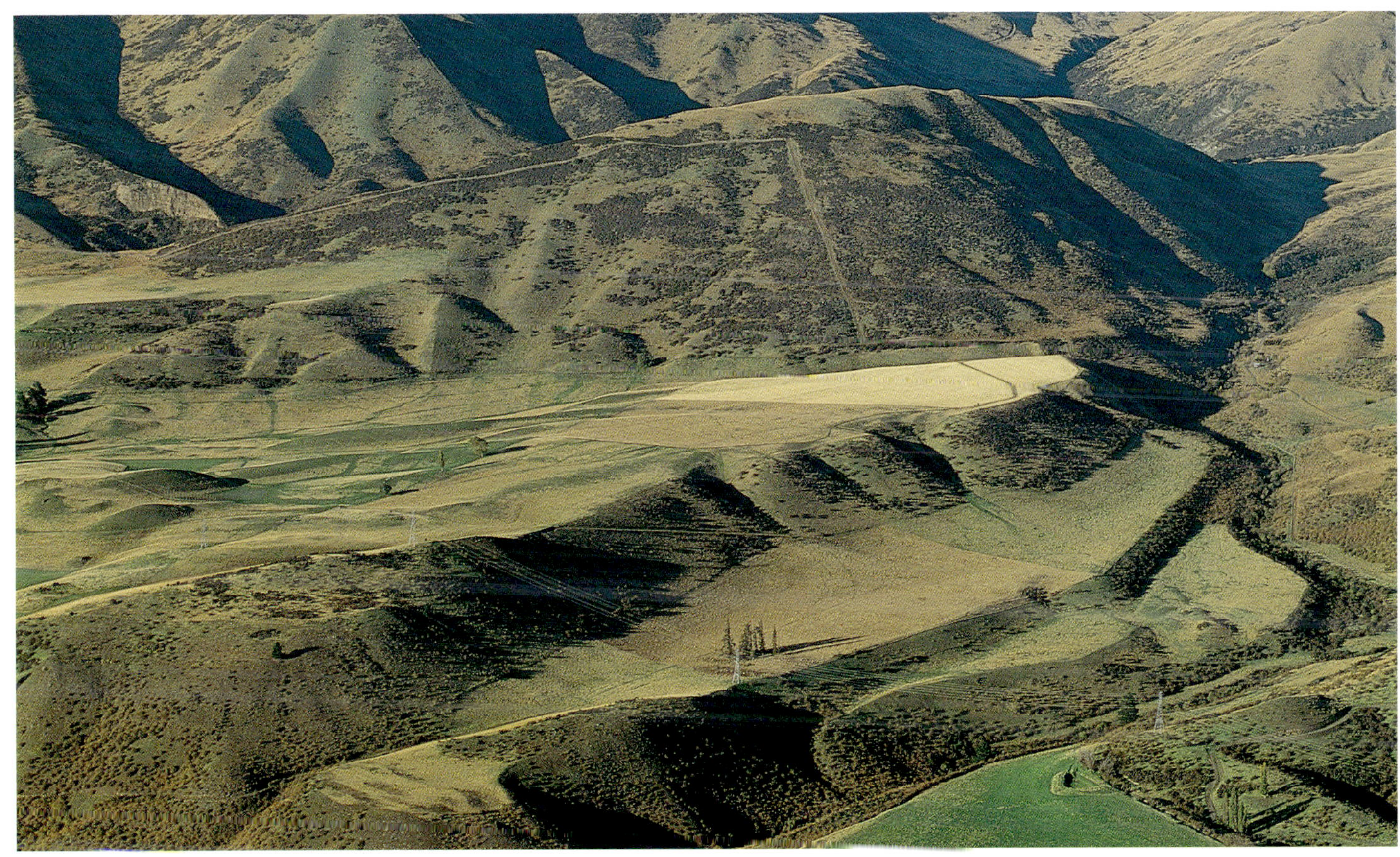

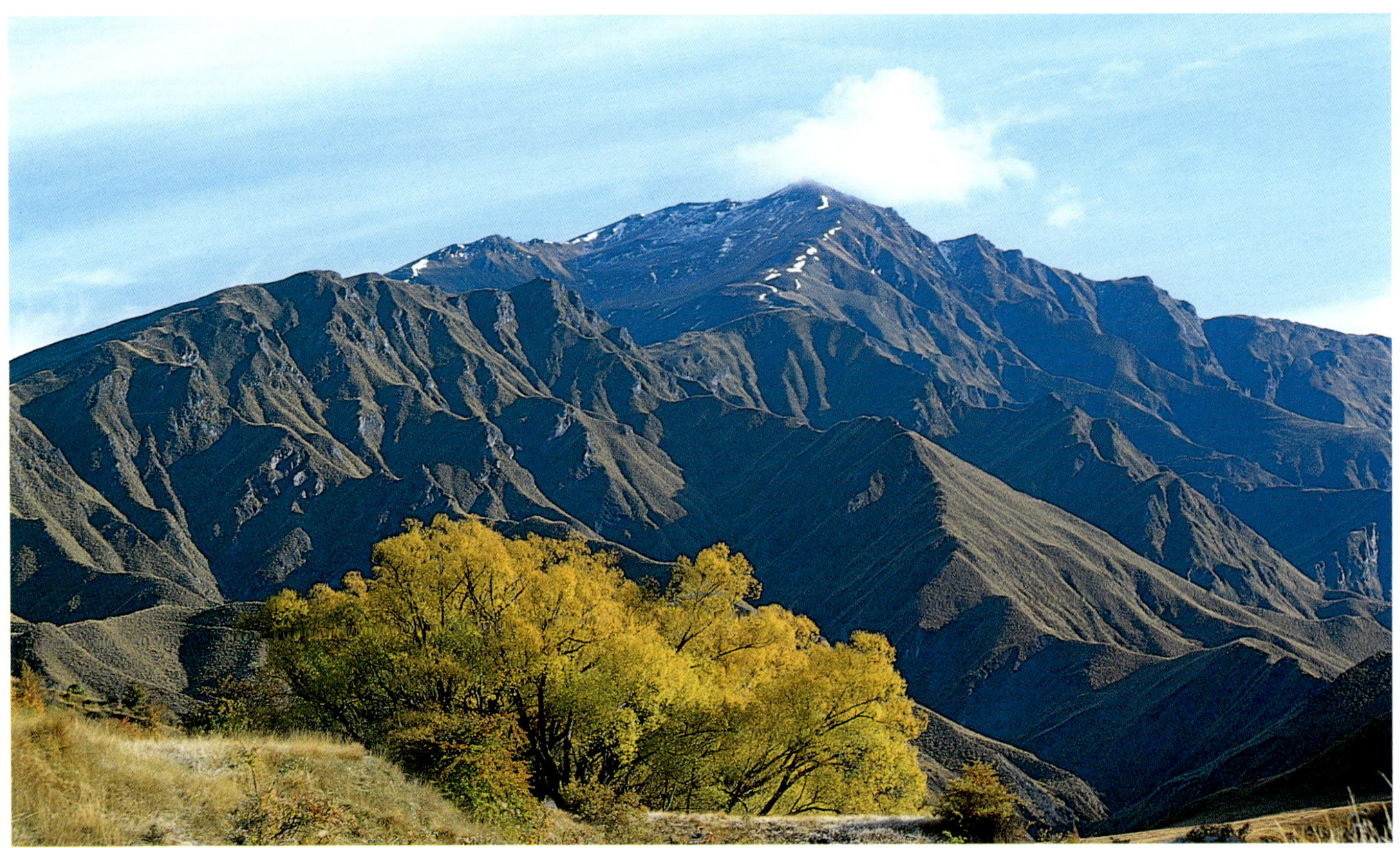

Macetown

The crisp frosts and blue mountains accentuate the glory of autumn colour on the drive to Macetown.

The Arrow River

We drove into Macetown on a sparkling, frosty morning when the grass was still frozen in bunches. The turquoise water reflected in the cliffs. We had 22 river-crossings to make before we reached Macetown – and this was our first at the Arrowtown water diversion.

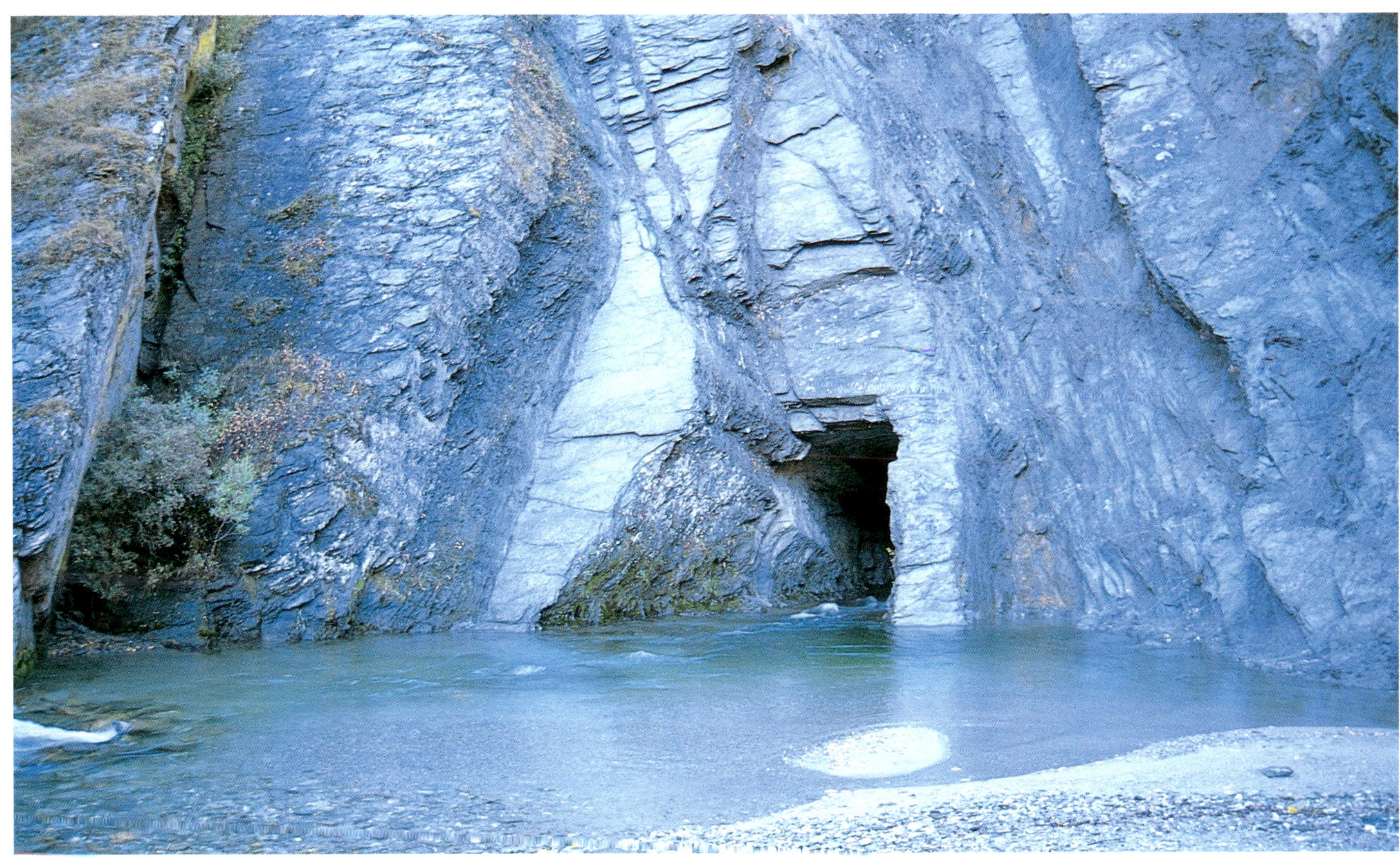

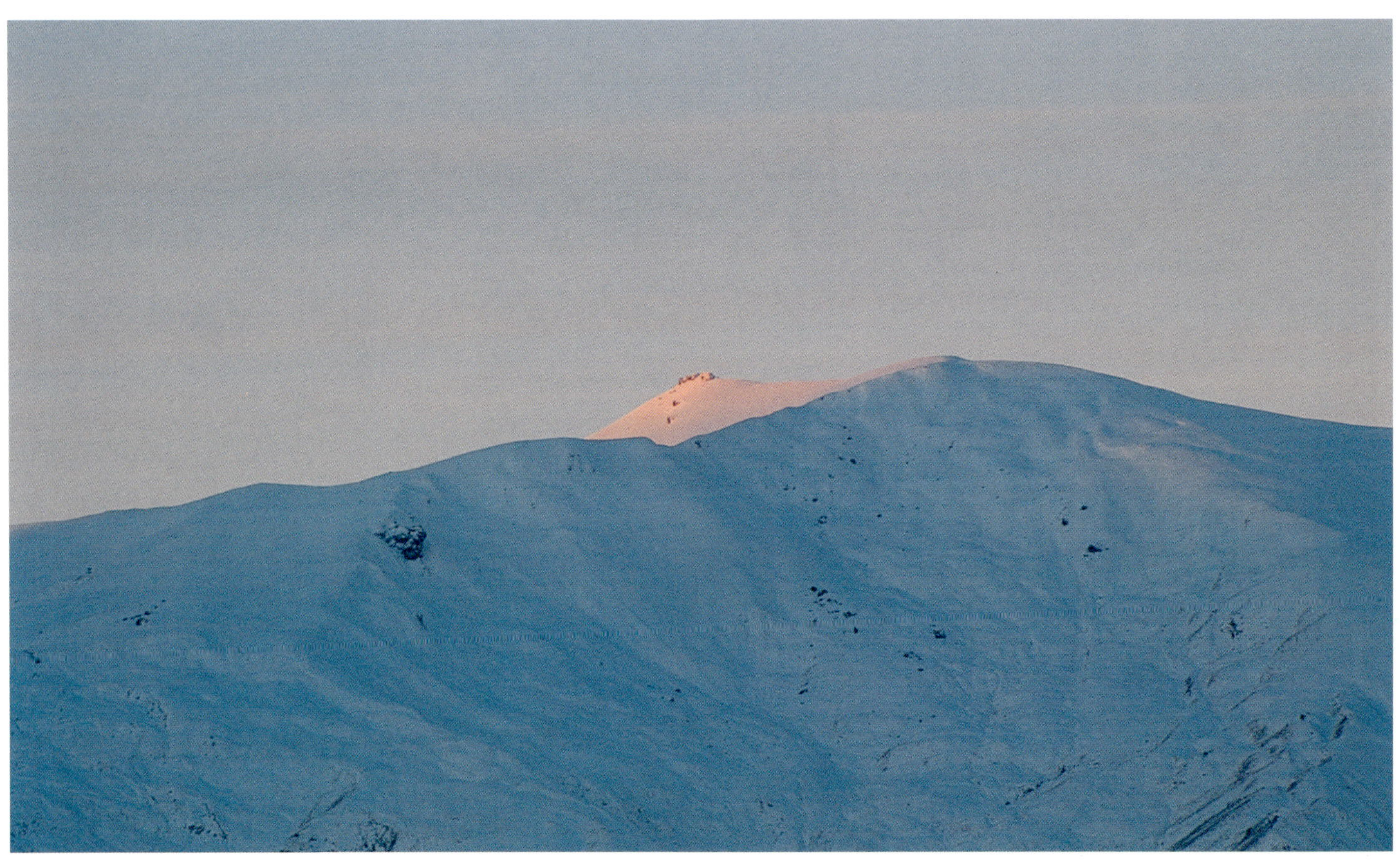

Spence Road

Here is the last light on the Arrowtown hills. One of the benefits of living in a campervan is that you can wait in comfort for moments like this. You can even have a rum or a mountain thunder (mulled wine) while you are waiting to take your shot. As a photographer, I find images like these hugely satisfying. You always know that they are special as you watch through the lens for that very last moment of light hitting the land. The hard part is the wait to see the transparencies.

Shotover River

Cold light accentuates the blues and golds of the lower Shotover River in the early morning. This was autumn at its peak and every time we turned a corner, the view blew me away. I took this shot from the bridge on the main road into Frankton, Queenstown.

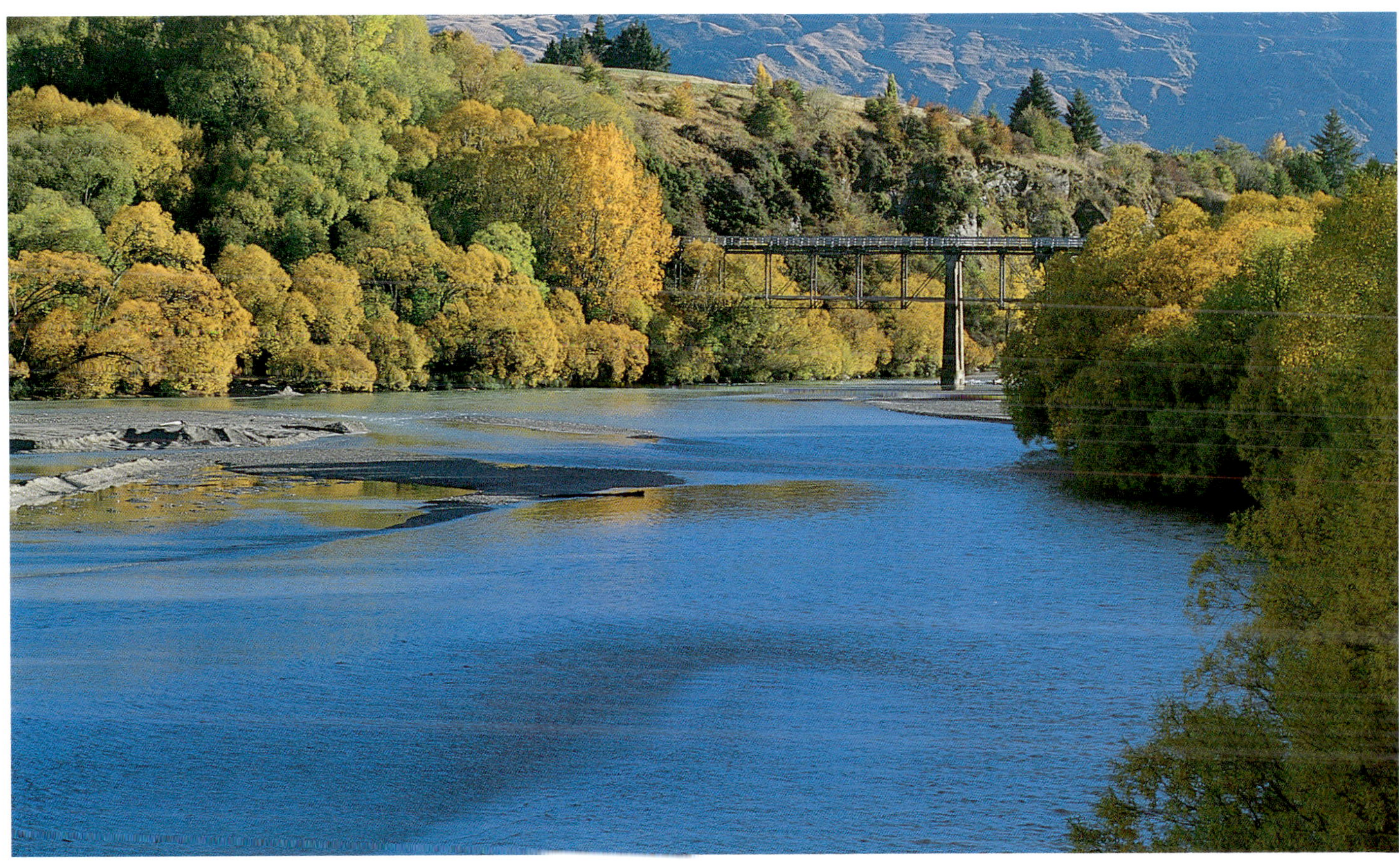

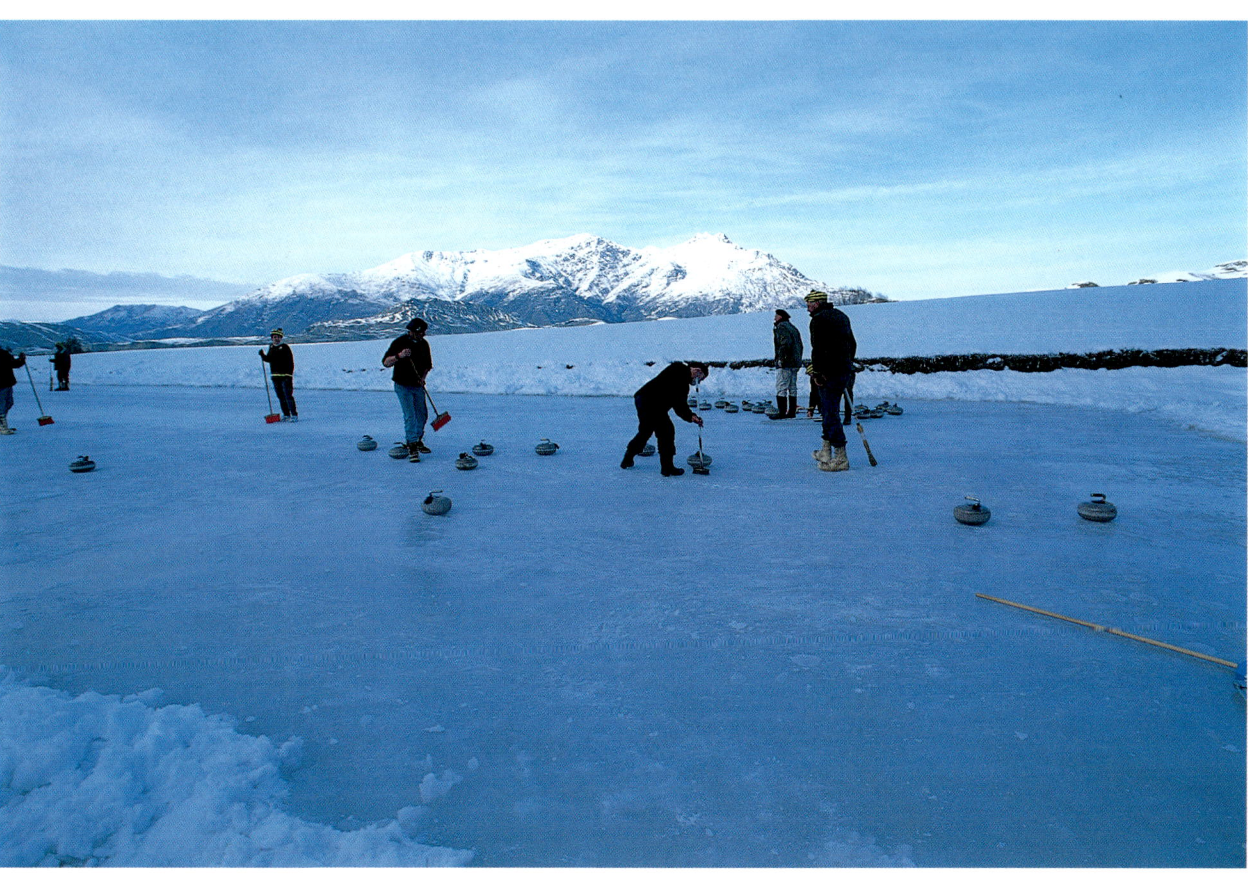

Coronet Peak

Having made a decision to revisit Southland and Otago after its largest snow dump in 25 years, I had two wishes. One – that the weather and snow would hold and two – I would discover people "curling". Blessed with fantastic weather and snow, I could hardly believe my eyes when Harry noticed a sign on a fence: "Curling". Sure enough, after a lengthy walk in the snow we came upon a tam-o'-shanter-clad team of Arrowtown curlers with brooms swishing and stones skidding along the ice.

Coronet Peak

Early morning sun back-lights the poplar trees and defines the hills at the foot of Coronet Peak where early snow has melted. This clear light lasted only a brief moment before drenching the hills and warming a chilly morning.

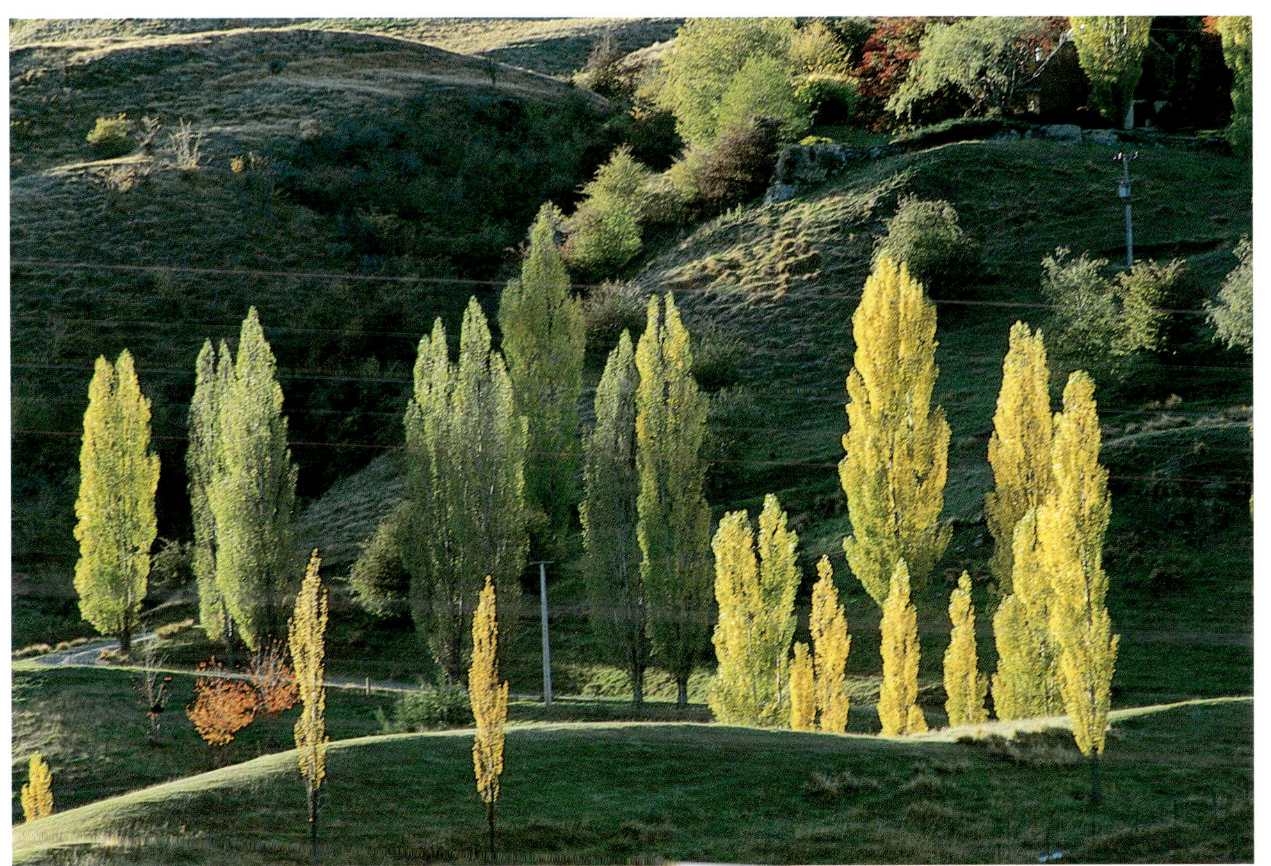

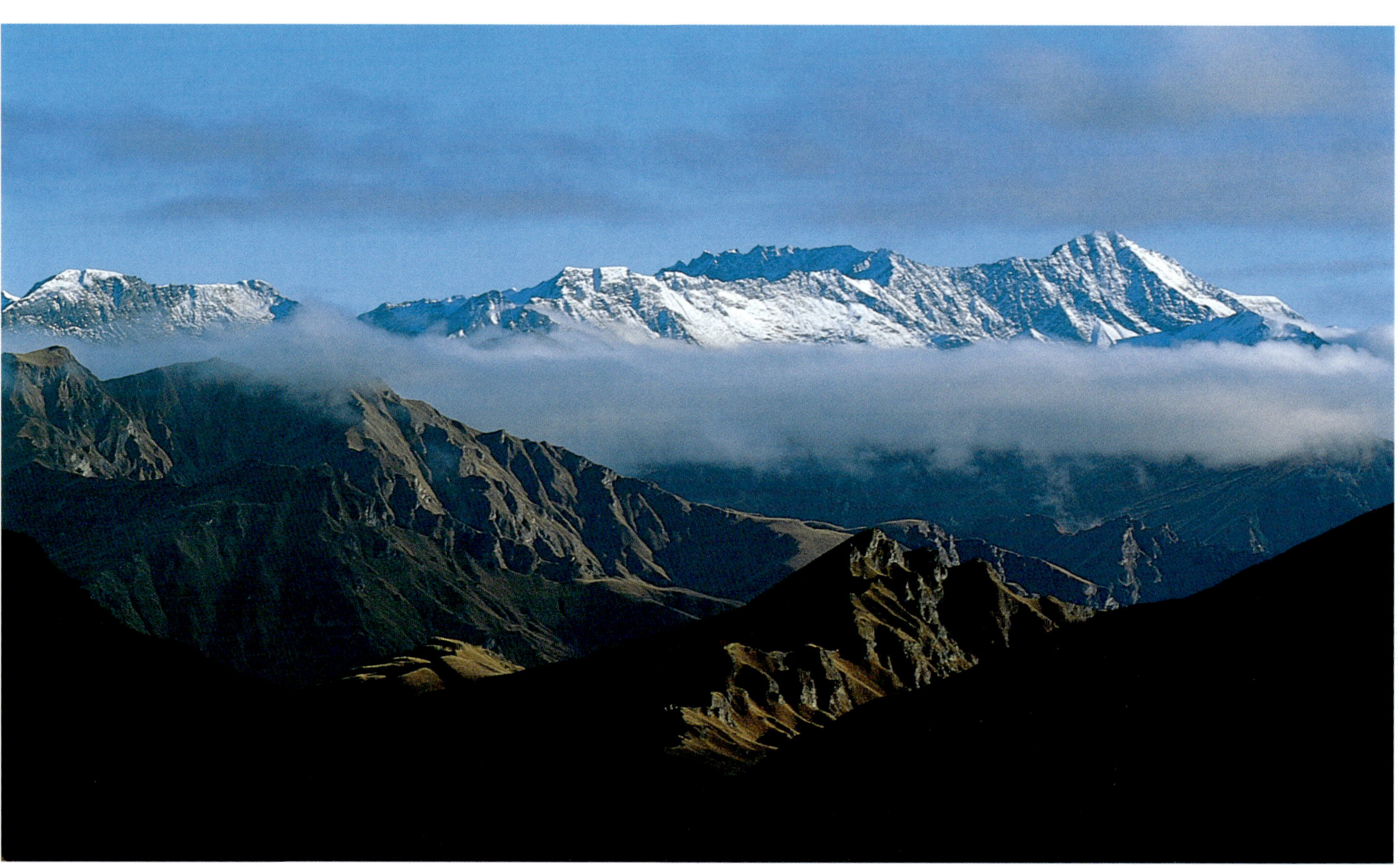

Skippers Canyon

The road to Skippers. Once again we were in the Nomad Safaris' four-wheel-drive with Kevin Reynolds. Snow-capped mountains that dominated the skyline and vast canyons filled with poplars and cold water were negotiated in comfort. Our journey was very different from those made by Julian Bordeaux, who carried supplies by horseback to the goldminers and their families every two weeks until he died on the track at the age of 87. This is a place of fascinating stories and breathtaking beauty.

Skippers Canyon

The Skippers canyon is framed by autumn fir trees. Caught by the sun, the water boils down this vast slash in the rocky terrain on its way to Queenstown and beyond. I marvelled at the strength and determination of those early travellers as I perched high up on the road they had hacked out of the cliff.

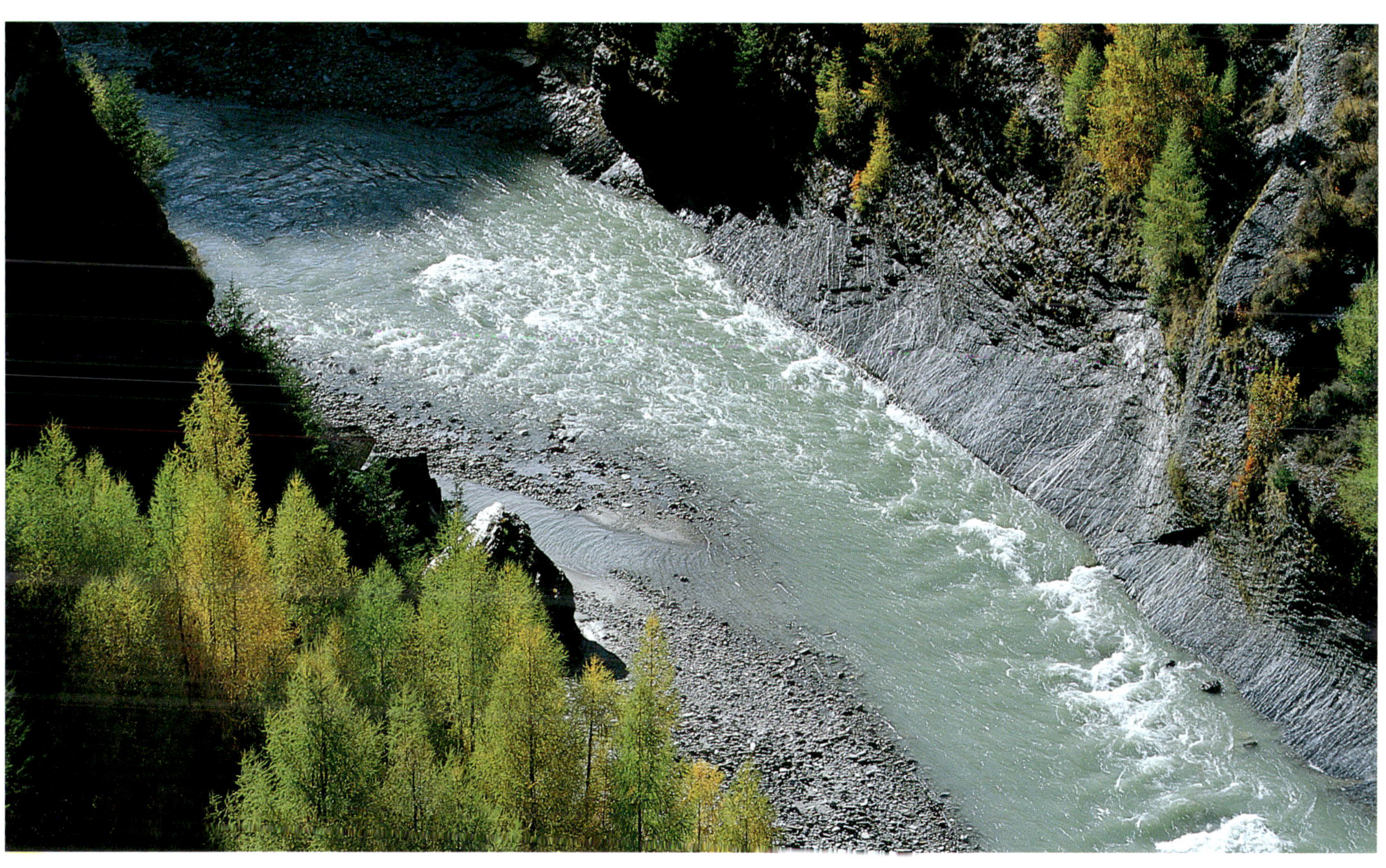

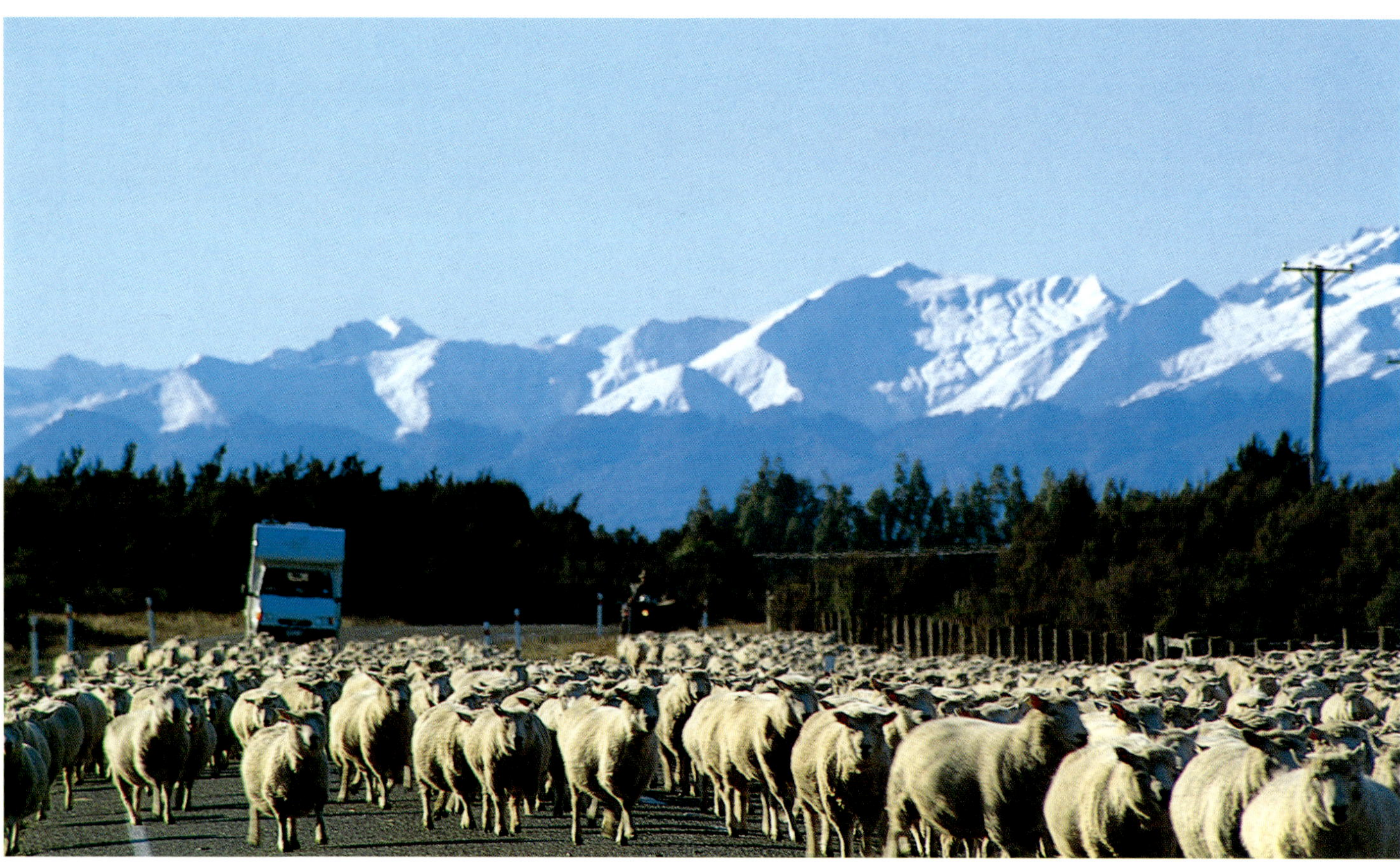

Te Anau

We revisited Te Anau in July after it had seen huge snow dumps. There was lots of activity on the surrounding farms as the lambing season began. In this truly New Zealand scene, we met 2800 sheep anxiously watched over by several tail-wagging dogs as they travelled to warmer lower slopes.

Milford Sound

The boat took us out to the Tasman Sea and we had a spot of fishing and saw a glorious sunset before anchoring for the night. I waited on deck in the morning in the cold and dark for first light, which struck the peak just as I pushed the shutter. The boat remained still for the millisecond I needed.

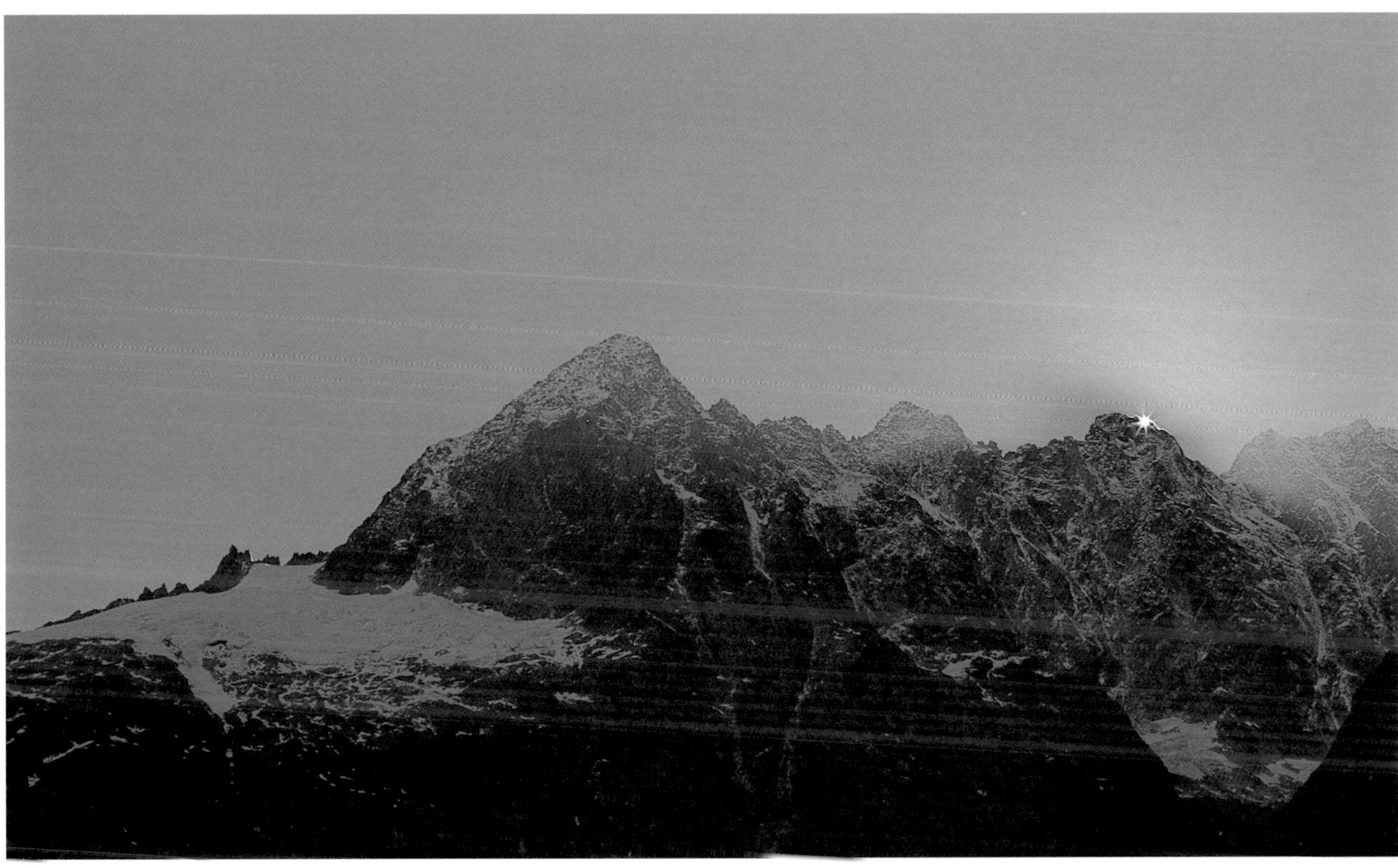

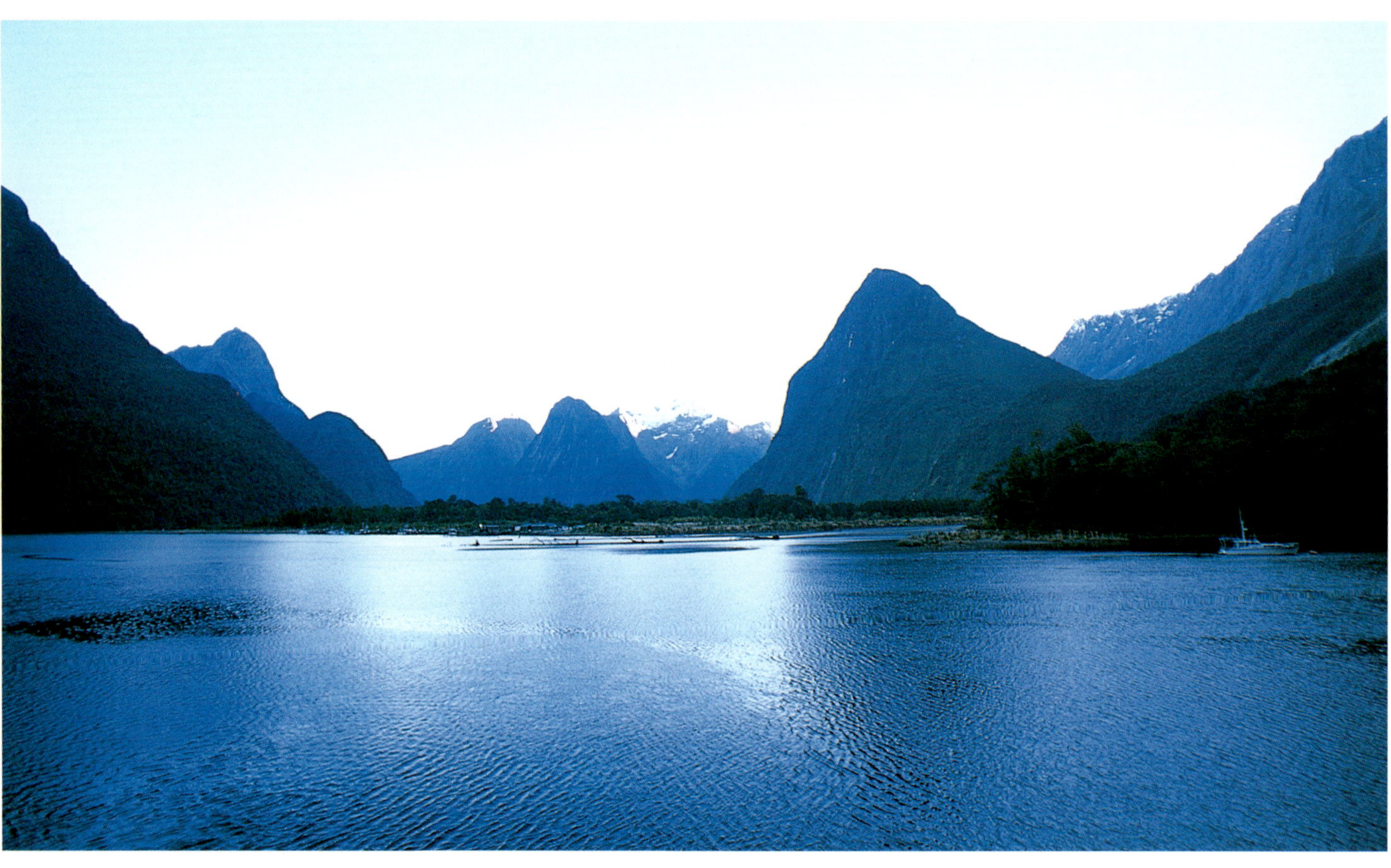

Milford Sound

Early morning on the Sound arrived in a cold blue light. It was my first visit to this tourist mecca. Thirty-four busloads of tourists were enjoying the scenery when we arrived. Here is my only travel tip – take a thermos and real food.

Fiordland

Soft greens, sunlight and the mysterious undergrowth in the early-morning light on the road to Milford. How lucky we are there's nothing to threaten, just birds with yellow breasts and black caps that all escaped my slow shutter speed. I will catch them in my next book.

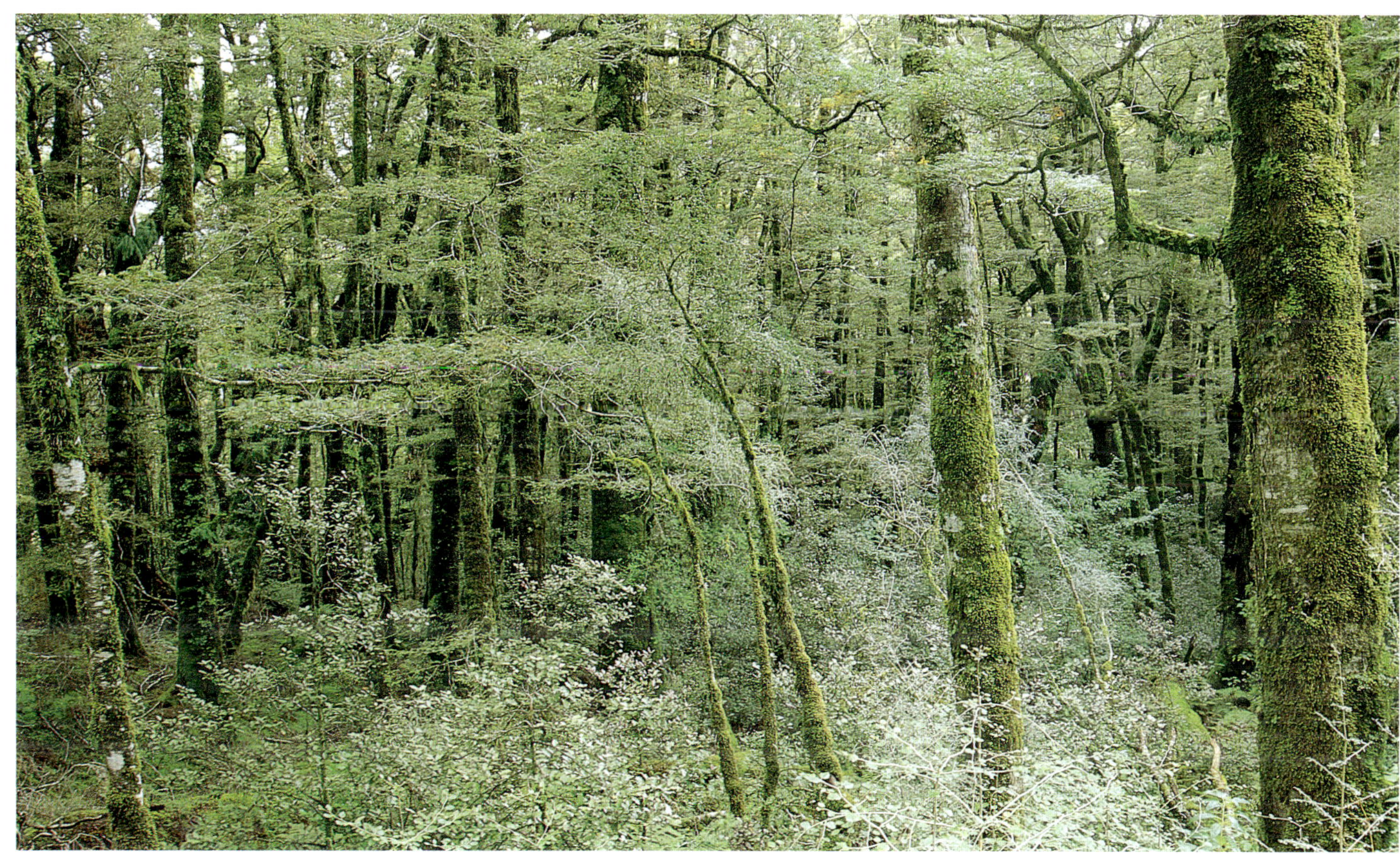

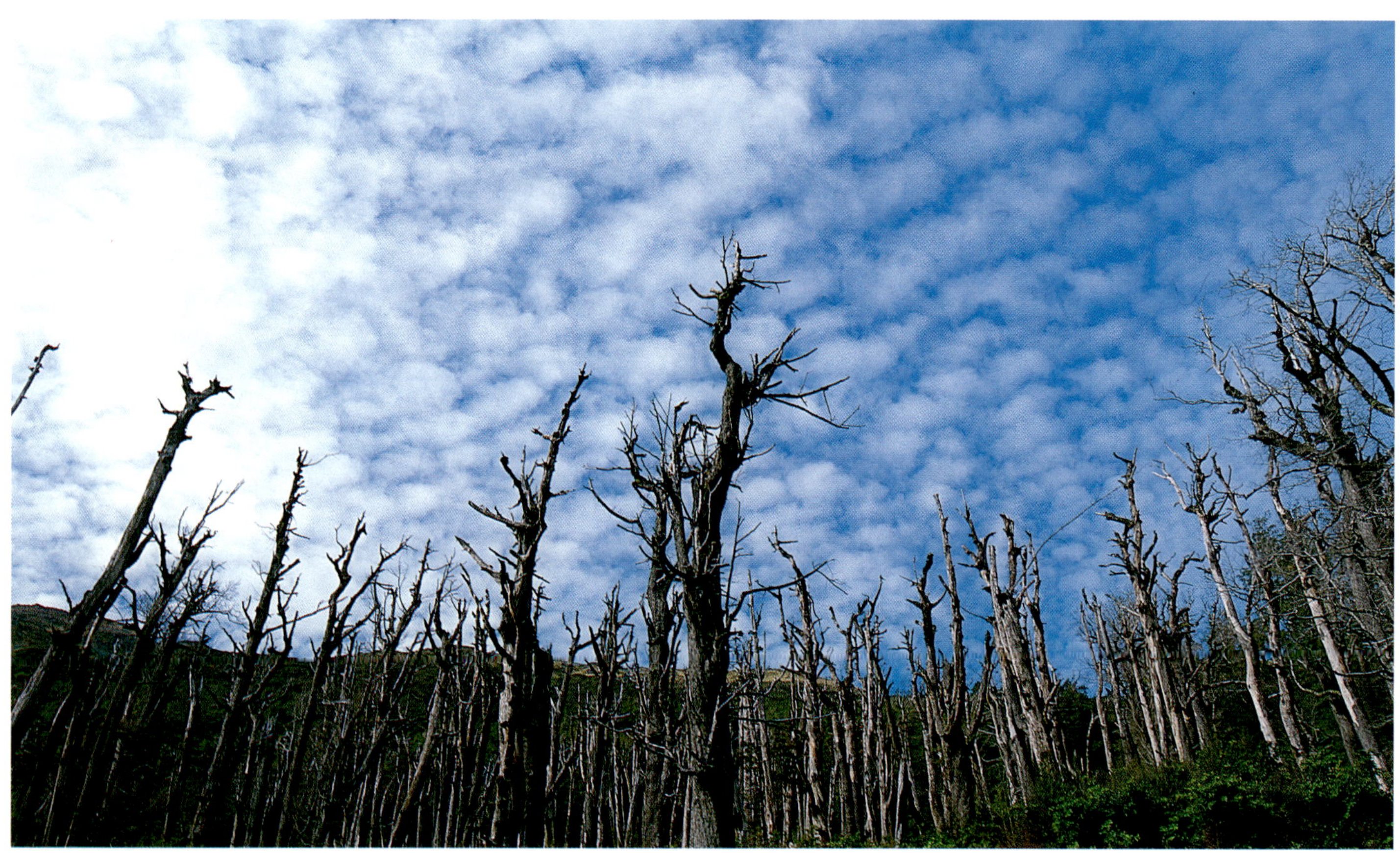

Lake Gunn, Fiordland

While the stillness of Lake Gunn provided wonderful reflections, I was fascinated by this lone group of trees providing a sculpture among the green of the Fiordland forest – while the sky added to this stark scene.

Southland

The Southland Scenic Route is stunning. The green land stretches to the blue ocean and the surf makes patterns on the pebbles that separate land and sea. Slope Point in the distance is emerald green against the blue and you can see Porpoise Bay where the surf was pumping up from the south.

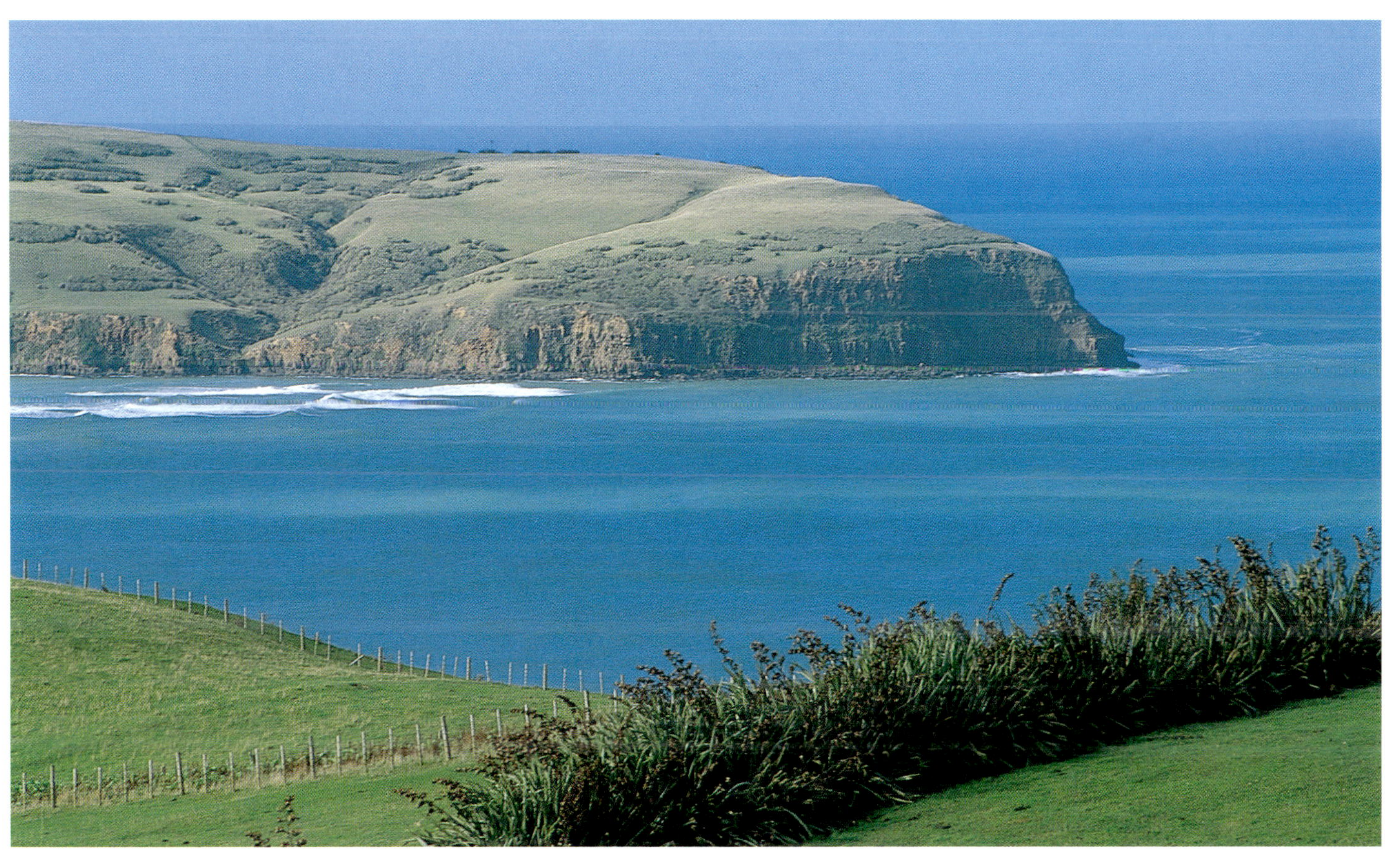

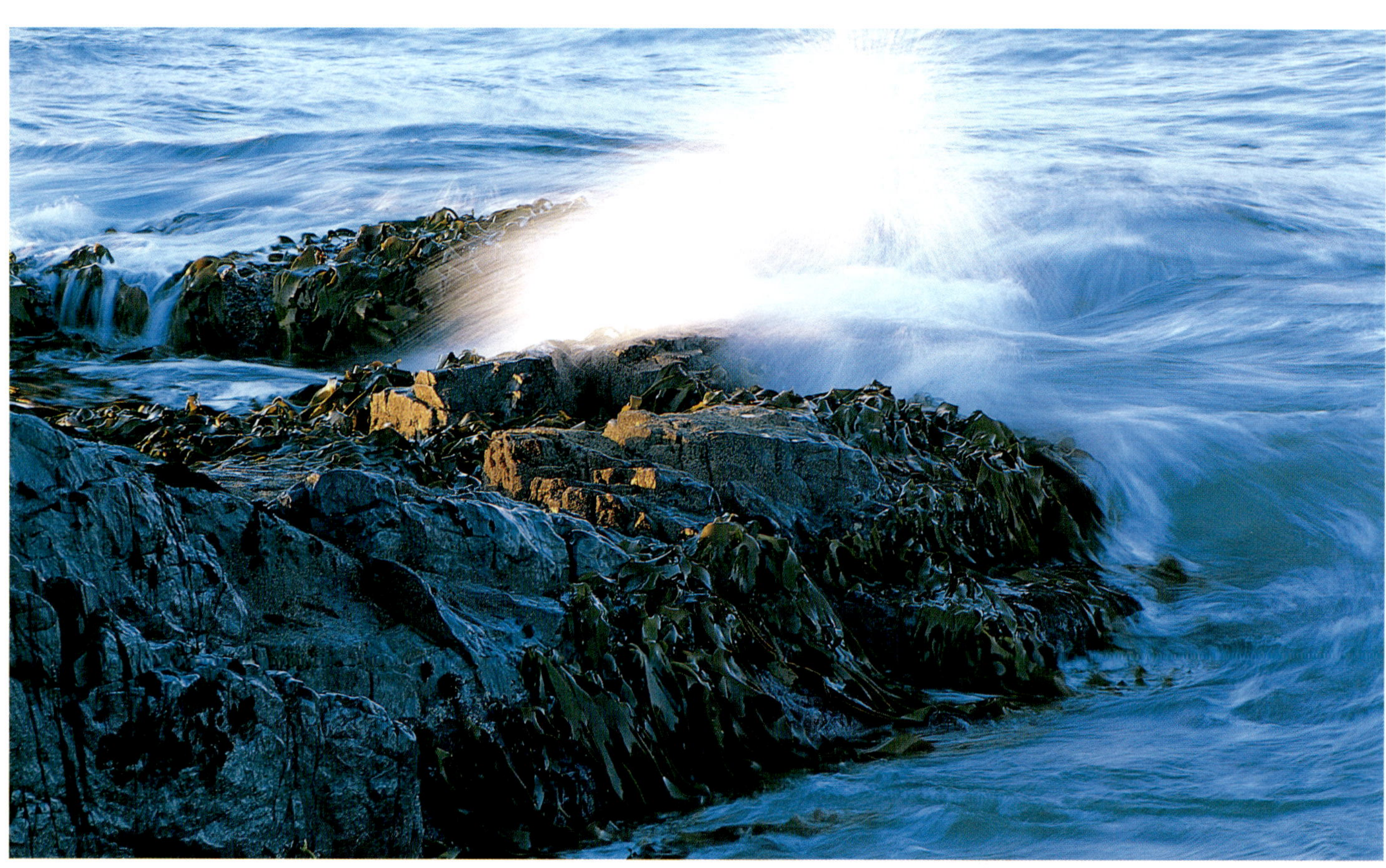

Curio Bay

Curio Bay on the Catlins coast. I love the way kelp moves with the tide and wraps itself around the rocks, making wonderful shapes and sometimes hiding seals. Andy Apse, my favourite landscape photographer, made some wonderful images of kelp that live in my mind. The sun strike in this shot makes it special.

Bluff

Early morning saw me at Lands End, which offers a wonderful view of Foveaux Strait, trying to shoot around the camper vans parked alongside the signpost. At that hour I could hardly knock on the door and ask them to move. My wait was motivated by the thought of the oyster boats returning. When they did, I was not disappointed as there is no other oyster in the world that tastes like a Bluff oyster. I've tested many for my friend Kel.

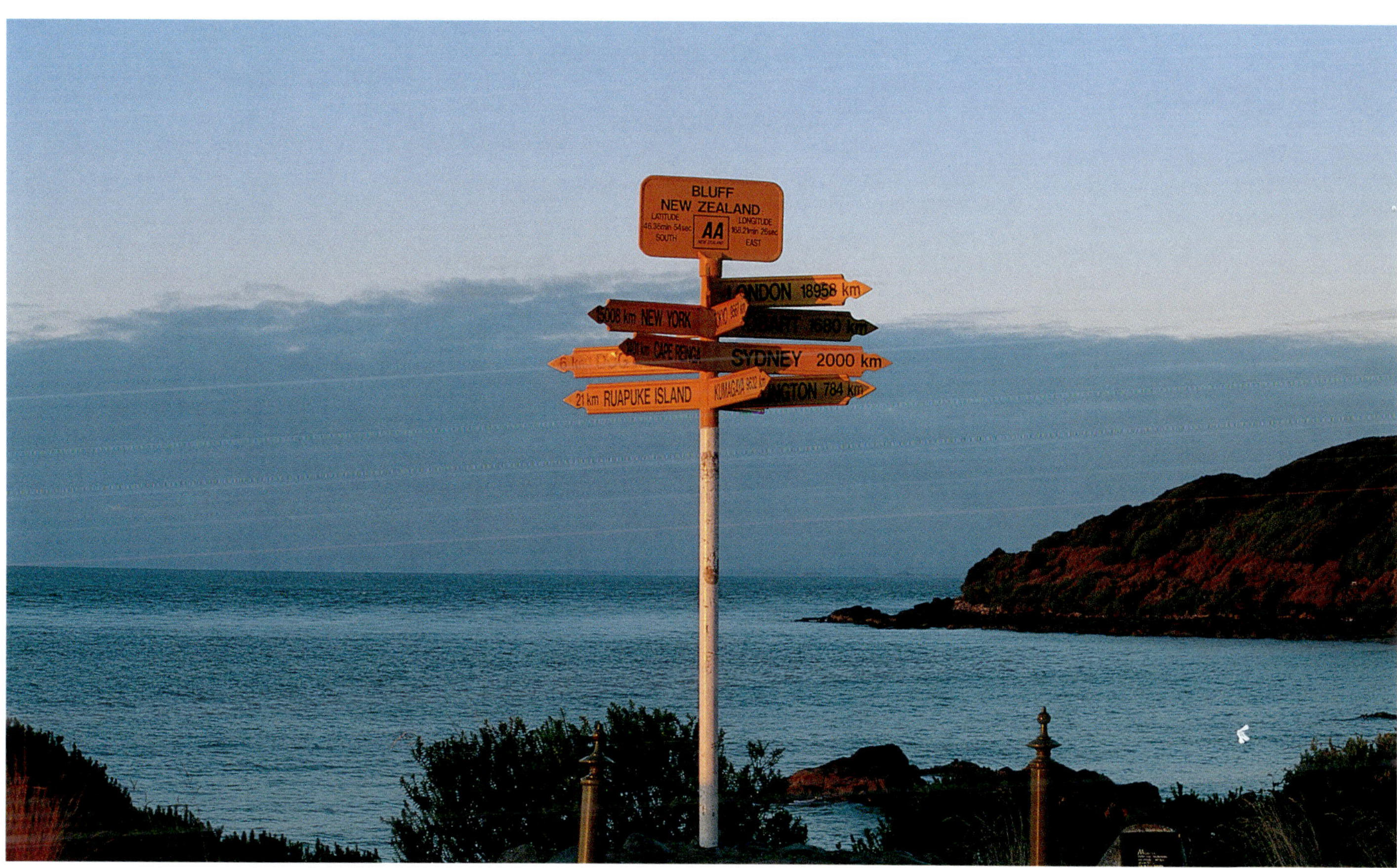
BLUFF
NEW ZEALAND
LATITUDE
46.36min 54sec
SOUTH
AA
NEW ZEALAND
LONGITUDE
168.21min 26sec
EAST
18958 km
NEW YORK
1680 km
CAPE REINGA
SYDNEY 2000 km
21 km RUAPUKE ISLAND
784 km

ISBN 1-86958-794-4

Published in 1999 by Hodder Moa Beckett Publishers Limited, [a member of the Hodder Headline Group]
4 Whetu Place, Mairangi Bay, Auckland, New Zealand

The film used by choice was Fuji Velvia
The original scans were done by P. C. L

Produced and designed by Hodder Moa Beckett Publishers Ltd
Colour separations by Microdot, Auckland, New Zealand
Printed by Bookbuilders, Hong Kong